Color of the Rainbow

Compassionate Leadership

Swami Amritaswarupananda Puri

Mata Amritanandamayi Center, San Ramon
California, United States

Color of the Rainbow
compassionate Leadership

Swami Amritaswarupananda

Published by
  Mata Amritanandamayi Center
  P.O. Box 613
  San Ramon, CA 94583
  United States

First edition by the MA Centre: 2015

In India:
  www.amritapuri.org
  inform@amritapuri.org

In US:
  www.amma.org

In Europe:
  www.amma-europe.org

Dedication

*This book is dedicated to
Her Holiness Mata Amritanandamayi Devi.
Her inspiring life, incredible wisdom and
incomparable example has always been my guiding light.
This book is her gift to the world,
my being only an instrument.*

Amma
Mata Amritanandamayi Devi

Contents

Preface   6

Foreword   7

Introduction   9

Chapter 1.   Management in the Embrace of Eternal Values   19

Chapter 2.   The Mirror Model   31

Chapter 3.   Celebrating Work   39

Chapter 4.   Virtuous and Vicious Cycles   49

Chapter 5.   Virtue, Equanimity, and Grace   59

Chapter 6.   Small Corrections, Big Changes   65

Chapter 7.   Needle and Scissors   77

Chapter 8.   Flowing Like a River   86

Chapter 9.   Contentment, the Real Wealth   96

Chapter 10.   The Hidden Strength of Sorrow   104

Chapter 11.   Multiple Lessons   115

Chapter 12.   Yet Another "Pyramid of Fortune"   130

Chapter 13.   The Power of Reverence   136

Chapter 14.   Ahimsa in Action   144

Chapter 15.   Aggressiveness Versus Assertiveness   151

Chapter 16.   Impenetrable Conviction and Instantaneous Decision   163

Chapter 17.   Guidance from Within   173

Chapter 18.   Love, the Purest Form of Energy   181

Preface

Swami Amritaswarupananda looks back through his 34 years with Mata Amritanandamayi Devi (Amma) and shares many deeply moving stories highlighting her unique decision-making, ideology, and pragmatic approach to the strategies and tactics that generate remarkable results.

Whether a scholar studying business theories at a university, a householder wanting to effectively manage a home, an employee who would like to develop the skills to manage others, or a business executive who has global employees to supervise, every lifelong student can benefit from learning the most effective concepts of management and how they are put into action. A vision that benefits society, fearlessness, motivation, hard work, adaptability, humility, compassion, discipline, forgiveness, gratitude, contentment, fairness, and patience all come to life in this in-depth study of Amma's ancient wisdom.

Chapter after chapter reveals practical ways of utilizing available resources, the right attitude one should have towards work, how to remain committed and responsible to projects we undertake, and above all the importance of maintaining a loving, compassionate, and detached attitude in everything we do.

Values are at the confluence of leading and inspiring. *Color of the Rainbow* highlights inimitable techniques to help managers intensify authentic loyalty and employee engagement while positively impacting society.

Foreword

The divine vision of Her Holiness Mata Amritanandamayi Devi, or Amma as she is fondly known around the world, could not have found better exposition than through the writings of Swami Amritaswarupananda. Having had the privilege of knowing Amma and Swamiji from close quarters and having drawn inspiration and moral courage from her teachings over the years, I am delighted that Swami Amritaswarupananda has decided to pen this book that eloquently puts to words the essence of the teachings of Amma. I believe that these lessons in management will be valued not just by her followers but will also find resonance and relevance with a wider audience.

Amma's extraordinary social service and humanitarian efforts have been legendary. Her aim to spread happiness and joy as God's message has changed the lives of millions. Her life has been an inspiration. Though she was herself far removed from the formal education system, she has been a successful architect of a remarkable network of humanitarian and charitable activities, whose expanse ranges from education to health services, social welfare and disaster relief. To manage all these activities, one needs management techniques which are of an exceptional quality. Swamiji brings to the fore Amma's teachings and her own inimitable and instinctive management wisdom, which has made her touch and transform the lives of millions.

I have long believed that management is more than managing a set of people, taking a company towards the path of profit maximization, leading a set of professionals towards attaining pre-decided goals, or fulfilling personal ambitions. Managerial ability stems essentially from inner strength, from being anchored in yourself as you deal with others. The knowledge in this book is sure to guide you to the possible sources of this inner strength. Swamiji's book looks into both the practical and the spiritual side of management. It is by combining both these elements that Amma's message has been spread around the world. This volume will allow readers to further their management skills and use them in ways to make a real difference to the world around them.

I congratulate Swami Amritaswarupananda on publishing this book on management. I am sure that this book will be a valuable addition to the already invaluable legacy of Amma which has brought so much joy and hope to people's lives around the world.

Shashi Tharoor
Member of Parliament
Minister of State for Human Resources Development
Former UN Under-Secretary-General

Introduction

Before I introduce this book, let me confess that I do not have a degree in management. I am not a professional manager, but rather, I am a monk. To be more precise, my life and work are under the guidance of a very special world leader. She runs her global organization using well-designed management principles, thereby teaching by example.

Her education is only up to the 4th grade. She speaks only *Malayalam*, her mother tongue. Her language is simple and colloquial. Nevertheless, she communicates with people from every walk of life, every level of education and experience, every caste and religion throughout the world. Her knowledge about the world, the people in it, and the human mind is astounding. Even the most intricate subjects are vividly presented through simple examples and stories.

I have been learning from her for the last 34 years, and I am still her student. Her name is *Mata Amritanandamayi Devi*. Her followers and admirers across the world lovingly call her *Amma*, and she is known for her distinctive way of receiving people by embracing each and everyone who comes to see her. She has initiated a vast network of charitable activities such as hospitals, educational institutions, research for societal transformation, disaster relief programs, vocational training, environmental programs, free homes for the poor, orphanages, and much more.

This book is an attempt to give an insight into Amma's distinct way of managing one of the world's largest NGOs. The entire credit goes to Amma because she is the soul inspirer and guide behind this work. For me, this was a long cherished dream come true. I still remember so vividly—it was just after Amma's 50th birthday celebrations (*Amritavarsham50*) that I first had the desire to write such a book. I told Amma about my wish. She said, "Go ahead." Since then, every once in while, Amma would ask me, "Haven't your eggs hatched yet?"

Well, I sat on the idea for many years. Actually, I have been mentally preparing to write this book for the last five years while reading books and articles, collecting information and, most importantly, observing Amma from the perspective of a Chief Enlightened Overseer (CEO) because, ultimately, it was her vibrant examples as an exceptional leader that accelerated the process and gave wings to my thoughts.

Close association and constant observation of Amma reveal an array of unparalleled skills: the calm and compassionate way Amma deals with all situations and problems; her immense patience and capacity to empathetically listen to one and all; her humility and equal vision; her informal way of mingling and communicating with people; the love and concern she expresses to all; and her inexhaustible energy. Managers and leaders can learn much from her.

Even though ancient Indian scriptures speak extensively about administrative and management systems, Taylorism or '*scientific management*,' as expounded by Mr. Frederick Taylor, was the first modern documented management trend. This approach emphasized study and measurement of the work being done, evaluation of the methods used, and assessment of the resulting productivity with little regard for the individual worker. The second movement began in America when Peter Drucker became a management guru. Dissimilar to Taylor's thoughts, Drucker's opinion was that although companies had a responsibility to earn a profit, they also had an obligation to take care of their workers. He pointed out and firmly believed that the workers need to be treated as contributing human beings, not as machines. Drucker's approach was later impacted by the Japanese style of management, which emphasized Total Quality Management (TQM) or Zero-Defect Management.

The models for management kept changing over the years to stay current with the surrounding political, social and economic environment. For years, the standard management model was the POLC Model (Planning, Organizing, Leading, and Controlling). However, due to improvements in communication technology and increases in the number of large-scale changes in the business environment, the ROAR Model (Reacting, Organizing, Awakening, and Re-visiting) has replaced the POLC Model in the past decade.

Today, the modern term used is Sustainable Management, a concept that confronts the problems of our times with business strategies. Also, organizations are seriously contemplating introducing democratic decision-making into the system, giving more freedom to employees with regards to selecting team leaders, other members, and workflow. The employees become more accountable in an atmosphere of friendliness and openness. Going beyond the traditional hierarchical structure, these organizations find this principled management style offers the best results. Such a structure could become the norm in the future.

Spiritual courses and workshops on yoga and meditation are offered with the hope of creating a tension-free, relaxed environment within the employee community. Creativity is positively impacted, and brainstorming sessions about new projects and ideas invites participation from all the stakeholders.

In today's world scenario, it would be accurate to say that most companies have their own management and leadership style, usually a conglomerate of ideas amalgamated throughout the hierarchy over many years. With the increasing number of interpretive commentaries on management and leadership, each company develops its own priorities, preferences and inclinations.

Management plays a vital role in all areas of life, not just in business and organizations. Wherever people strive together to achieve a common goal, we see principles of management either in a subtle or gross form. Amma observes, "Whether it is five people living in a house or five hundred people working in a company, ultimately management means managing minds. It can either be five minds or five hundred minds. But the most crucial point is, unless you learn to manage yourself, your mind, thoughts and emotions, how will you be able to effectively manage others? This is the first and foremost lesson—learn to manage yourself."

In Amma, we can unmistakably see the very best modern management concepts such as a vision that truly benefits society, fearlessness, motivation, hard work, adaptability, humility, compassion, discipline, forgiveness, gratitude, contentment, fairness, patience, etc. Watching Amma sitting hours on end embracing people, reporters all over the world ask her about the secret of her tireless energy. Amma's answer to them is, "I am not like a battery that would die away after using for some time. I am eternally connected to the power source."

A in-depth study of this multi-dimensional leader will reveal practical ways of utilizing available resources, the right attitude one should have towards work, how to remain committed and responsible to projects we undertake, and above all the importance of maintaining a loving, compassionate, and detached attitude in everything we do.

There is a well-known story about the great sage Veda Vyasa. He authored the eighteen *Puranas*, the *Mahabharata*, the *Brahmasutras* and codified the Vedas. Being a wise and enlightened soul, Vyasa had foreseen the future of humanity. He realized that in the following ages, mankind would plunge into the deep quagmire of spiritual, moral, and ethical degeneration. As a selfless benefactor of the world, he wanted to do something for his unfortunate descendants. Hence out of sheer compassion, he first codified the Vedas and divided them into four parts. Thereafter, he composed the Mahabharata. This phenomenal composition alone consists of over 100,000 verses, over 200,000 individual verse lines. Each verse is a couplet. The word count of the book is about 1.8 million words. This is roughly ten times the length of the Iliad and the Odyssey combined. The studies and the enormous research work he had completed were like holding a minimum of one hundred PhD's, real mastery over a vast variety of subjects.

Vyasa genuinely believed that his works would uplift the coming generations. However, he could still see humanity enveloped by darkness. So, even after all these unique compositions, the astonishingly brilliant sage felt a deep unhappiness, which was, in fact, a reflection of the misery of future mankind. To find a solution for his perplexed state of mind, Vyasa approached another great being, sage *Narada* and sought his advice on the problem. Narada advised Vyasa that the main reason for his discontentment comes from the absence of true love in his compositions. Although an awakened soul, unequalled in knowledge, he did not infuse aspects of divine love in his masterpiece works. Narada told Vyasa that more than knowledge, what the future generations would need is the experience of true love that reveals the oneness or unity of the God-principle. Inspired by Narada's advice, Vyasa wrote the great epic, the *Bhagavata Purana*, depicting Sri Krishna's life, childhood pranks, and on top of all, the unconditional love the cowherd girls had for Krishna.

The story is filled with meaning and profound messages. One: our life and all our achievements are pointless if we don't have a sense of deep and reverential love toward all of creation. Two: we may have a long list of accomplishments, but none of them are the summit. The peak of existence is love. Three: awakening the dormant love within and realizing it is our innate nature elevates us to the state of pure compassion. When the heart is filled with love, it overflows as compassionate words and actions. If not all, at least it benefits the maximum number of people around us. Four: even though Veda Vyasa himself was a repository of divine qualities and incomparable wisdom, he was humble enough to seek the advice and blessing of another great sage, Narada.

Now let us look at these ideas from a business point of view. When we hold a high office, power, and position, it is obligatory on our part to show maturity and understanding in word and deed. If it is not our nature, we will have to develop it. Otherwise, it is not economical. It will affect our career. So, a reverential attitude is important. In life we cannot stand still. If there is no forward movement, soon we will be pushed far behind. It is like a humongous crowd of people running. We have no other choice but to run. Or else, we will get trampled on. So, keep running with the crowd, but at some point take off and soar to greater heights. Is there any fun in repetition? The fun is in ascending, rising up in love, not to keep falling in love. When we rise in love, we gain more maturity and understanding. We will start seeing everything from a higher plane of consciousness. A new light of compassion and consideration dawns. This leads to the state of humility, which in turn activates a continuous flow of pure energy within and in all our actions. When we bow down to the universe, it flows into us.

Imagination, creativity, and innovation, the three vital factors for success, happen only when we love life, when we develop a worshipful attitude towards work.

Love is only lust for the people who dwell solely on the physical level. For those who are able to go beneath the surface on the mental level, love is imagination and creativity. For them, love is a feeling. Great dancers, musicians, painters, and poets go into a trance, a temporary identification with that which is being created. Ralph Waldo Emerson was correct when he explained, "A painter told me that nobody could draw a tree without in some sort becoming a tree; or draw a child by studying the outlines of its form merely . . . but by watching for a time his motions and plays, the painter enters into his nature and can then draw him at every attitude . . ." This type of love is a deep feeling that lasts for some time. It indeed is rare and precious. Then there is a third category of people who realize, "I am love." Love is a constant experience for them. In such love, the prison created by 'I' and 'you' on either side of 'love' disappears. There is only love.

The enormous work and tremendous contributions of the ancient Indian seers, Aristotle, Plato, Homer's Iliad, and Odyssey are examples of the unimaginable heights and accomplishments a man can reach in one life time! This was possible because they discovered the source of pure energy known as undivided love within. This source of unconditional love is the secret of Amma's inexhaustible energy and the success she has achieved.

Vijay Bhatkar, the architect of India's national initiative in supercomputing says, "It is Amma who inspired me to undertake the initiative of building supercomputers. Amma not only emphasizes the importance of the Intelligence Quotient (IQ), but the Emotional Quotient (EQ) and Spiritual Quotient (SQ) as well. Thus she creates a balance between scientific, spiritual and cultural education. Amma has revived the language of love and compassion. This language is universal and eternal, comprehensible to all beings in all times. In Amma's expression, love and compassion get magnified to superhuman dimensions, hitherto unseen. While hugs are common between parent and child, intimate friends or lovers, Amma's hug is universal, transcending nationality, race, language, religion, age, or station in life.

"Some years ago, the famous linguist from the Massachusetts Institute of Technology (MIT), Professor Noam Chomsky, discovered that there is a language-processing center in the brain, which facilitates the processing and learning of languages. This center understands only meta-language, which is like the language behind all languages. In a similar way, Amma has brought forth the common denominator among all linguistic traditions, the language of love and compassion. It is through this universal language that Amma is able to communicate with anyone, regardless of where they are from. Although she only speaks Malayalam, Amma is able to communicate with all her children; we, too, are able to communicate with her, sometimes through silence. This is yet another one of Amma's unique contributions to the world."

Inaugurating the Amrita Institute of Medical Sciences & Research Center, a state-of-the-art multi-specialty hospital started by Amma in 1998, Sri Atal Bihari Vajpayee, the then Prime Minister of India said, "The world today needs solid proof that our human values are useful, that such qualities as compassion, selflessness, renunciation, and humility have the power to create a great and prosperous society. Amma's work provides us with the much-needed proof."

I remember a story as narrated by one of Amma's followers who had been asked to spend a few days video taping the poor people in their original homes before they moved into the new homes Amma had built for them. "There was a woman. I don't really know her story: an old widow, with earlobes elongated by heavy jewelry long since gone, no doubt to make ends meet. Before getting into the car, I looked back and grew still with wonder. There, in the age-old tradition of India, as night was falling, the ancient woman was lighting a lamp in the doorway. She did it entirely by feel, for she was blind—a blind woman lighting a lamp for those who can see."

'I am Love, I am God's effulgence in a human form;' this knowledge will serve as an inexhaustible source of energy. All professed successes amount to failure if we fail to be a good example to the future generation. Our name will be inscribed in the annals of history, but our thoughts and actions will neither be admired nor respected. Hence, in addition to acquiring external knowledge, health, and wealth, all leaders should also aspire for internal knowledge, inner health and internal wealth. Balancing these three factors is essential to achieve real growth and success, which will be remembered forever. I sincerely hope that my efforts to recapture and share Amma's inspiring life and work through this book, will benefit the reader and arouse the urge to emulate her example at least to some degree.

I would like to express my heartfelt gratitude and sincere thanks to Sneha (Karen Moawad) for her dedicated efforts in helping me edit this book, to Swami Paramatmananda for doing the inside layout, and to Aloke Pillai (Toronto), a young and talented artist who did a wonderful job of designing the cover.

Swami Amritaswarupananda
Mata Amritanandamayi Math
Amritapuri, Kerala, India

Chapter One

Management in the Embrace of Eternal Values

In today's world when people hear the words, 'management or leadership,' they immediately associate these terms with managing a company or political leadership. Basically management means overseeing resources, finances, priorities, and time. In business, ultimately, everything boils down to profit, the surplus that can be taken home to increase the bank balance.

Even though management and leadership are generally attributed to only certain selected areas of life, it is also part-and-parcel of our everyday life. Whether in a small roadside village teashop or a five star hotel, in a hut thatched with coconut leaves or a palatial home, management principles inevitably come into play. We live in an age of the nuclear family, friends sharing an apartment, or just one person living alone. Nevertheless, leadership and management have a vital role. Just as there are leaders and managers in a company, there are leaders and managers in a home.

Technology has changed the way we live and is creating a serious gap between generations. Many homes have been technologically converted into offices. Prominence is given to technological skills and logical analysis, especially by the younger generation. Parents may have the power to take decisions in the office, but at home, children are the decision-makers because they are greater information gatherers than their parents regarding modern digital systems. They are not only good at collecting knowledge but they excel at updating systems and information as well. As parents try to catch up, conflict ensues.

Our markets are flooded with products. Every six months to a year there is a newer model of mobile phones, laptops, iPads, tablets, cars, motorbikes, and what not. In truth, people are now so stressed because they 'need' so many of the newly developed gadgets in order to be happy. Their desires are 'out of control.' I'm not being pessimistic. We all sense our own misalignment with regard to desires, but we don't want to change our old patterns, our deep-rooted habits. However, simple corrections in our life and outlook can bring about miraculous changes. We just must have the willingness to do it.

It is like the ancient concept of '*maya*' (illusion). The definition of 'maya' is that everything is neither real nor unreal. Maya exists within and without. Inside it exists as thoughts and outside as objects. We are constantly being tossed between the never-ending waves created by these two worlds, the inner and outer.

Things are in a constant flux. People are waiting to throw away older models and run after new ones. With innumerable choices, people are confused. These conflicting desires affect both family and professional relationships. Take a deeper look into the definition of 'maya' and humanity's present condition. Observe the behavior of the people around us. Falling an easy victim to the fascination created by the world of technology, are we not trapped in a world of illusion?

People everywhere, even in villages, have become more health conscious. We see them going for early morning walks and jogging. In cities, over 60% of the population have gym memberships. Yet there is a rapid increase in mental illnesses, hypertension, high blood pressure, early diabetes, heart disease, etc. Why? It is simple logic—people have fewer moments of restfulness. They spend more time brooding, becoming anxious, desiring 'things' and craving what others have. The test of good mental health is freedom from disturbing thoughts and emotions that would upset our inner equilibrium.

In life, both manmade rules and the ever-existing mysteries of the universe, the law of the unknowable, are equally important. Gravitated by the pull of habits and behavioral patterns, we forget to keep this balanced view. It doesn't matter if we are poor, rich, educated, or illiterate, a CEO of a multinational company, owner of a small scale business, or a farmer, knowledge of these two aspects and practicing them in all our dealings is the key.

Life is the greatest of all games. Our ability to keep these the man-made rules and the law of *dharma* in perfect balance is what determines our success, happiness and peace in life. Viewed with discerning eyes, winning the game is not the end goal. True victory is in winning it with nobility. Giving too much reality and importance to both worlds is dangerous. So, be centred in the middle. Neither be this side or that side. From the middle, the center, we will get a pretty good view of everything, whereas inclination will only give us partial views.

This is where spiritual thinking, self-introspection, meditation, and a kind and compassionate attitude can open up an entire new world around us. So let me suggest a formula: 1) Introspect daily, 2) Detect your weaknesses and limitations, 3) Overcome them, and 4) Replace negative thoughts with positive ones. A change of vision happens only when we realize our weaknesses and transcend them.

Governments and multinationals have succeeded in enhancing the comfort level and standard of living for everyone. Economic success in the world seems to have improved. At least that is the impression created. However, if that is the case, why is there so much discontentment and agony? Why has bipolar disorder amplified at such an alarming rate? Why have the number of suicides all over the world increased? Why are conflict, violence, war, hatred, and selfishness on the rise? It seems we have tried every power available in the world (economic, military, intellectual, scientific, and technological) with little or no positive result.

As a society, we are improving in terms of science and technology, but we are disintegrating mentally. Along with these scientific and technological advancements, the mind must also advance. Otherwise, science and technology will only serve to bind us. Ultimately, they will only lead to our suffering.

Parents, teachers, and people who can influence impressionable minds should have the maturity and understanding to correct the perspectives of our children. We are all fully aware that our children are going to be responsible people in the future. They will be husbands, wives, grandparents, managers, professionals, politicians, etc. Just as we support them for their education, we should teach them how to handle their desires, their mind, as well as their actions and reactions. Tell them not to allow their desires to become greed. Tell them intense craving and deep hatred will cause a real threat to their inner peace and joy. Teach them the value of honesty, truthfulness, compassion, love, caring, and sharing. Most significantly, parents should know that discipline is not enough. Children must see their parents as good practitioners of these positive qualities, even if they are not perfect.

But, as we grow up watching what our elders do, we learn a different message—that taking advantage of others leads to success. We get the wrong idea that we can adopt any means to attain our goals in life by cheating, being dishonest, deceiving others. By example, adults teach children to cover their tracks and close all loopholes so that they don't get caught. The inference is that the more cunning they are, the more successful they will become. Society also teaches that being loving and compassionate is a sign of weakness.

People in today's world, particularly youngsters, think that spiritual principles, or the eternal values, are nonessential. But, if we closely observe our everyday life, all of us practice these values in our interactions with situations and people. We just don't call it spirituality. For example, when you carefully listen to a person's problems, you are being spiritual. When you sincerely sympathize with someone, you are practicing spirituality. When you show compassion to a beggar or a needy person, it is nothing but spirituality. When you are concerned about the welfare of your employees, you are certainly being spiritual. In a similar manner, when your heart melts looking at an orphaned child, that, indeed, is spirituality. But, do we call this spirituality? No, we don't. We call this normal, right? Yes, spirituality teaches us to be ordinary and to live like normal human beings.

Unfortunately, today when a student graduates from a university such as Harvard, Princeton, Yale, MIT, or from one of the Indian IITs, or IIMs, the understanding is that the goal of life is *kama* (expensive car, big house, home theatre, the latest smart phone, etc.). To fulfil these desires, we need money and success. People make money and become successful—one justifies the means—and says that it is all *dharma*, righteousness. For example, people take a bribe and say that it is dharma to take a bribe because the pay is low and everyone else is taking bribes.

As a result, real freedom—freedom from tension, stress, and all kinds of negative and destructive thoughts—is nonexistent as is the cause and effect relationship between desires, money, righteousness, and freedom, which are completely reversed from what they should be.

In many cities around the world, it is said that to live a life with social status and comfort, we need the Five C's. They are cash, car, credit card, condominium and club membership. But we forget about a sixth one, crematorium, a guaranteed C. Whether or not we achieve all the first five C's, the sixth one will definitely come, irrespective of country, nationality, power, and position. There won't be any prior notice or warning. It just snatches us, and everything that we claim as ours, away.

You may think that this talk about death and cremation are irrelevant in this context. But, I disagree. Whether we believe in the theory of rebirth or not, death is indeed significant because it is such a major event in our life. While busily engaged in managing our life, business, and all the other factors to win a victory, we often forget about death, the absolute failure of the ego that can befall on us at any moment. Nothing can stop it. So, remembrance of death is important because it makes one feel humble. And humility is an essential quality for those who wish to win and succeed.

We live in an e-world: e-learning, e-reading, e-governance, e-commerce, e-business, e-library, e-seva center, e-banking, etc. The list is endless. Keep all those E's since they are beneficial to society. But completely avoid one E, a dangerous one: Ego. That E should GO. At least keep it under control. Don't allow the ego to enter and interfere without permission. If you feel it is necessary, permit the ego to enter and once the purpose is fulfilled, show the ego the 'exit' door.

As normal human beings working in a world of stress and cutthroat competition, it is not easy to achieve our goals in life. Pause and reflect deeply upon what your goals actually are. Have you prioritized them? What do we really need in life? Along with name, power, position, and assets, are not happiness and love indispensable aspects of life?

Success, which is said to be an important goal in everyone's life, really boils down to happiness. Many people chase money in order to buy happiness. At regular intervals, you might ask yourself:

1) Is my happiness level rising or falling?

2) Do I have love within, and am I able to genuinely express it outwardly?

If your answer to these questions is 'yes', your life is moving towards success. If the answer is 'no', then you are just making money. A true leader will not consider economic gain as genuine success without love and happiness being inseparable aspects. Ultimately, a good leader should contribute to making people happy. An unhappy leader with no love to share can only make people suffer.

"Happiness is not something that happens. It is not the result of good fortune or random chance. It is not something that money can buy or power can command. It does not depend on outside events, but rather on how we interpret them. Happiness is, in fact, a condition that must be prepared for, cultivated, and defended privately by each person," as explained by Hungarian psychologist, Mihaly Csikszentmihalyi, noted for his work in the study of happiness and creativity, but best known as the architect of the notion of 'Flow'—a state of heightened focus and immersion in activities such as art, play, and work.

Expanding one's business, opening branches all over the world, and making a profit might be desirable. But, alongside, we should also attune our minds to tap into the unchangeable laws of the universe. This is essential to generate a positive change in the attitude of human beings. This change will raise the level of happiness and peace for each one of us and for future generations as well.

All the material progress and profit we make is ultimately meaningless if the world becomes a place where two people cannot live together in a happy and loving atmosphere. Just observe a family of two living under one roof when they are at each other's throats. How can humanity lead such a superficial life? We have had smart management gurus, scientific geniuses, great thinkers, writers, and political wizards, but what if we don't have the skill and will to manage our own inner world, our mind and emotions. What use is there if we fail to create a balance between our head and heart or between the craving to amass wealth with the desire for happiness?

It is clear that we need good role models in our world to encourage a change in values. We can't do much about the previous generation. The current generation is intelligent and smart but already has set behavioral patterns. A true inspirer can create an impact on the current generation. Decisions and visions have already been made, but there is tremendous potential in the growing-up generation. A true inspirer can positively influence the current generation and truly transform the growing-up generation.

Mata Amritanandamayi Devi, or Amma as she is fondly known around the world, is an exceptionally compassionate spiritual leader and humanitarian. This book offers her management approach based on the wisdom of the ages. It describes the way Amma sees life from a different dimension and how she manages situations and resources, takes decisions, and inspires people.

Since 1993, Amma has been increasingly recognized by the international community as a treasured repository of practical spiritual wisdom who has the capacity to guide the world towards a better, brighter future. We greatly need masters who can teach us by example, people who are natural managers, scientists, artists, and virtuous politicians. The light they shed is, indeed, the need of the hour.

Although educated only up to grade four, Amma is the founder, guide, sole inspirer of, and the catalyst behind a worldwide network of humanitarian activities, including health care facilities and educational institutions.

Amma has a special way of meeting or welcoming people. Referred to as *darshan*, she embraces each person by helping him or her to experience the transformative power of love, the joy of giving, and the gift of caring and compassion. Amma's darshan emerged as a loving mother's hug, beginning when she was only a teenager and held and comforted the lonely and suffering in her village. Amma makes herself available to anyone wishing to receive her warm embrace. No one is turned away. Hour after hour, day after day, year after year — for over forty years now, she has been embracing all who come to her. Man or woman, sick or healthy, rich or poor, young or old, regardless of religious faith or caste, regard her as their very own Mother. Amma now travels across India and to countries throughout the six continents. Everywhere she goes, she gives darshan to all who come to her.

In India, Amma has been known to individually embrace over tens of thousands of people in one day, sitting sometimes for over 25 hours. Over the past forty years, she has embraced over 33 million people! Each person's darshan is a fresh experience because Amma herself is ever fresh, ever spontaneous. Amma listens to us, hugs us, and whispers a word or two in our ear. She knows exactly our need of the moment. With a pause here, a glimpse there, she instils moments of transformation. This is the testimony of thousands.

Amma says, "My religion is love." Reporters ask her, "Why do you hug?" Her patient response is, "The question is like asking a river, 'Why do you flow?' I simply can't be otherwise." To the question, "You sit and hug people hours on end? Who hugs you?" her answer is, "The entire creation hugs me. We are in an eternal embrace." Seeing the large number of people who come to receive her iconic hug, reporters sometimes ask her, "Do these people revere you?" Her reply is, "No, I revere them."

Amma says, "True love transcends all barriers. It transforms and is universal." These simple principles, put into action, are the basis of Amma's life. But the impact is profound. Healing and transforming the hearts of millions of people across the globe, Amma's life stands as a testament to the truism 'Love conquers all.' Her life is the ultimate success story—living proof that it is possible to transcend all barriers and obstacles, be they gender, religion, language, caste, finances, or education to create balance and harmony throughout humanity.

Amma says, "The values of love, compassion, concern, honesty, truthfulness, humility, and forgiveness are now almost like a forgotten language. Thankfully, they are just 'forgotten,' not 'lost.' Like a mirror covered with dust, these values remain deep within us but hidden. We just need to dust ourselves off, and we will rediscover the mirror of compassion, our true nature. In fact, we learn many lessons about these values from our parents during our childhood. In almost every home, we hear parents telling their children, 'Son, don't ever lie. Always tell the truth. Be fair to your brother or sister. Don't take that iPad; it is your brother's/sister's. Be honest...'"

The ideas, the perspectives, and the special leadership qualities depicted as you turn the pages of this book may not be appealing to an organization focused entirely on profit margin. Amma's ways may be inimitable, but indeed, she is a magnificent model and immensely inspirational. The approach described in this book can be a tremendous source of power in managing both your inner and outer worlds if the reader is willing to study the examples and adopt the management style described.

Chapter Two

The Mirror Model

The *New York Times* featured this article in its May 25, 2013 edition:

"In fact, Amma has energized an entire organization that often fills the vacuum left by government. When a tsunami devastated parts of southern India in 2004, it took the state government of Kerala five days merely to announce what it would do by way of aid and relief. Amma, however, began a response effort within hours, providing food and shelter to thousands of people. In the following years, her organization says that it has built more than 6,000 houses. She has built a vast organization that is the envy of both India's public and private sectors. They said she'd built a place where everything, from light switches to recycling plants, worked as it was meant to — and, in India, this was perhaps the greatest miracle of all."

'*The Khaleej Times*,' one of the leading daily newspapers in Dubai, UAE (United Arab Emirates), highlighted the following article in its December 9, 2011 edition:

"*4th Grade Dropout Leading Brain Drain Reversal*"

"Prime Minister Dr. Manmohan Singh's call to Indian scientists living abroad to return to India to help the country break into the big league of developed countries did not bring many despite many incentives, but a woman, who has studied only up to 4th grade, is bringing some of the best brains back. The much-touted reversal of brain drain is being catalyzed by Mata

Amritanandamayi, who has emerged as one of India's leading spiritual leaders by breaking caste, social, economic, educational and several other barriers. Amritanandamayi, who is popularly called Amma, has been attracting top scientists from across the world not by throwing huge sums of money but by impressing upon them a higher sense of service."

How does she do this? What are her main tools? The techniques she uses are not new. They are the age-old tools of Love, Compassion, Listening, and Patience. Amma is the consummate practitioner and creator where the reward includes peace, happiness, and contentment as well as material prosperity. I refer to this unique methodology as the Mirror Model:

1. **Meditation:** Finding the silent spot within, transmitting that into action by sincerely listening to the problems and queries of team members, and giving guidance and direction without losing clarity, patience and equanimity. This doesn't mean we should sit in *samadhi* 24 hours a day, but it is an inner capacity to let go, to withdraw, and to remain aloof from the crowd of people and thoughts in order to contemplate on concerns until the shell that covers the solution breaks. To illustrate this with an example, I would use the mother hen sitting on her eggs until they hatch and the baby chicks are born.

Amma says, "With all that is happening in our world today, the only way to stay sane is by making meditation part of our daily life. Our professionals are yet to learn the wondrous benefits that meditation can bring to them. An entire world of unexplored treasure remains unopened within, but sadly, nobody wants to open it even though the key is left with us. We miss beholding the brilliance of that immense treasure as our thoughts and negative emotions build huge barriers between us and the fortune within. It is like standing in front of a celestial flower but not seeing it."

When meditation is mastered, the mind is unwavering like the flame of a lamp in a windless place.

—Bhagavad Gita, Chapter 6-19

2. **Intuition:** Once we realize the silence within through meditation, then it is not the mind and its conflicting thoughts that guide; we develop another faculty, an intuitive mind which enables us to take the right decisions at the right time with the right understanding.

Even with all the advancements in science and technology, with all the sophisticated equipment at hand, there are times when neither the mind nor the intellect can provide us with the answers we seek. Moments are frequent when even the most brilliant brains are immobilized and stuck, unable to move forward. We have made maximum effort, done everything, and now things pause in a state of cessation. This is when we need the help of intuition, a faculty that connects us with the unknown source of knowledge.

Amma says, "To be intuitive means to be spontaneous. The first step towards being spontaneous is effort and hard work. The second step is to let go, forget all that you have done, and be in the present, in a restful state of mind. From that restfulness emerges the third step, and the intuitive mind begins to function."

Steve Jobs, a luminary of our time, said, "Your time is limited, so don't waste it living someone else's life. Don't be trapped by dogma which is living with the results of other people's thinking. Don't let the noise of others' opinions drown out your own inner voice. And most important, have the courage to follow your heart and intuition."

3. **Responding rather than Reacting**: Response and Reaction are two different ways of looking at a situation or person. Response is a natural and relaxed state of mind. It is more of an allowing, an opening up. A responsive person has more understanding. This helps us to consider situations with a non-judgmental attitude, which leads us to new avenues of knowledge. In response, we see what others don't see. Our unprejudiced approach makes our decisions more accurate. This attitude has a positive effect on our productivity. In fact, response-ability' is the ability to respond.

Conversely, a reactive person's mindset has a relatively imbalanced aspect to it. Anyone or anything can make him or her upset and agitated. You will find him on the verge of exploding. Most importantly, since a reactive person's mind often loses its calm, the decisions he or she takes will lack precision.

In fact, by reacting, we invite our competitor to win because reaction makes us vulnerable. On the other hand, response is the trait of a mentally strong person who has better control over his emotions.

If a situation demands, response allows anger to surface consciously, but the emotion doesn't subjugate us. Reaction allows anger to overpower us with the result that our actions will not have the proper awareness.

Mostly, we view people, situations, and objects in light of our past experiences. We can't help but be judgmental. It happens unconsciously and is our second nature. What we really fail to understand is that when we allow our past to judge something, we actually are reacting, not responding. Reaction is from the past, and response is from the present.

How do we view our parents, family members, boss or coworkers? Rooted in our yesterdays, right? We have gathered too many impressions about them from the past. These old patterns are like a veil of smoke that prevents us from beholding them newly each moment. However, if we really think about it, wouldn't it be correct to say that every moment we take a new birth? Some things die in us, and certain other things are born. But when we view people with our mind fixed in the past, we don't see this fresh aspect of life. Aren't we losing something precious by not considering this side of people and things? To summarize the whole concept, a vast majority of us think we are responding, but in reality we are reacting because we always view situations and people from the storage space of our past memories. Thus, response rarely happens whereas reaction happens quite frequently.

Thomas Paine, an author, revolutionary, radical, inventor, intellectual, and one of the Founding Fathers of the United States, answered, when asked about anger management, "The greatest remedy for anger is delay."

Amma suggests, "When someone criticizes you, at least tell the other person, 'Let me sleep on it, and I will come back to you in a few hours. If what you said is true, I will accept it. Or else I will give it back to you.' Most probably, you will realize that the other person was right and you were wrong because you were in a reactive mode, and he was in a calmer state of mind and could step aside and be the witness."

There is a certain frequency, intensity, and recovery period for each emotional disturbance that is triggered. A rise in our awareness level will minimize these emotional disturbances. When we keep working on our awareness level, the time it takes to spring back to normalcy also diminishes. This awareness will eventually help to maintain calmness, cheerfulness and confidence at all times. As our inner capacity to return to the state of calmness attains depth, our whole thought process becomes much sharper, and our decisions will gain more accuracy.

4. **Oneness:** A sense of oneness between the employer and employee. The main factors that lead to this unity are a bonding born out of love and the power to listen. These two, 'love and listening' go hand in hand. A loving heart listens. Listening gives greater strength and confidence to team members. They open up, trust, and discharge their duties more as a dedicated service than just working to earn money and promotion. In this approach, there is no lack of co-operation, and each synchronizes the activity with that of the other. The entire team works together with mutual understanding to achieve the target goals.

Amma says, "God is not an individual who sits above the clouds on a golden throne passing judgments. God is all pervading pure consciousness, which is our true nature. So we all are one in essence. Just as it is the same electricity that manifests through a light bulb, fan, refrigerator, TV, and other electronic gadgets, it is the same life principle that connects everyone. When the left hand is in pain, the right hand automatically caresses and consoles it because both hands are part of one unit, our body. In a similar manner, we are not totally disconnected entities, living in an isolated world; we are all part and parcel of the universal chain."

As Fritjof Capra, a well-known physicist, pointed out in his book, 'The Turning Point,' "Quantum theory thus reveals a basic oneness of the universe. It shows that we cannot decompose the world into independently existing smallest units."

5. **Reverence:** This is not respect born out of fear but reverence born out of love. So, the employees have both respect and love for the employer. This reverence creates a comparatively friction-free working atmosphere both for the employer and the employees.

Amma says, "Teaching culture, heritage, and values must have a place in the standard curriculum to preserve the diversity lost through globalization. Along with subjects such as arithmetic and language, education in values such as love, compassion, and reverence for nature should form a part of the core curriculum. When we engage others with respect, understanding, and acceptance, then we will be able to communicate at the level of the heart."

As everything is pervaded by an undivided, intrinsic God Consciousness, a reverential attitude will uplift us to a higher plain of pure energy.

In the Mirror Model, the team has a zealous and inspiring role model at the head. By setting an example of love, patience, compassion, acceptance, perseverance, perfect control over emotions, and a friendly approach, the feeling of 'Otherness' is replaced with the feeling of 'Oneness.' The feeling of 'I Am' is replaced with the feeling of 'I Owe' to the world and my fellow beings. The feeling 'I Am Your Boss, so Obey Me' is replaced with, 'We are All Here to Serve, so Be Humble.'

Amma's extraordinary ability to listen to all sorts of problems and her amazing capacity to interact with people from all walks of life, from all over the world, is legendary. Tens of thousands of people come to see her wherever she goes. No matter how big the crowd is, Amma sits for hours on end, receiving each one of them in a warm embrace, regardless of gender, age, status or physical condition. She patiently listens to those who pour their hearts out to her. And each of these sessions lasts until she sees the last person in line.

Owing to her mother's ill health, Amma had to discontinue her studies after grade four. At that tender age, the entire responsibility of attending to the household chores fell on her shoulders. Amma speaks only Malayalam, her mother tongue. However, she communicates with people of all nationalities, languages and cultures with ease, and there are absolutely no strange feelings or a sense of otherness.

Every one of us has our own convictions about life and the goals we want to achieve. A thief's conviction is to 'steal.' A money-oriented person's is 'to make money by hook or by crook.' Similarly a gambler thinks, 'gambling is life.' Amma's conviction is, as she described in a speech at the UNAOC (United Nations Alliance of Civilizations) Conference in Shanghai 29th December 2012, "In my experience, the one language that humanity and all other living beings understand is Love. For the past 40 years, I have been communicating with people of all languages, races, colors, castes and religions, from the very poorest to the rich and famous through the language of Love. There are no barriers for Love. I have full faith in the transformational power of Love to unite all hearts."

Chapter Three

Celebrating Work

During an address delivered in New York on the occasion of the 50th Anniversary of the United Nations, Amma said, "This world is like a flower. Each nation is a petal. If one petal is infested, does it not affect all the other petals? Does not the disease destroy the life and beauty of the flower? Is it not the duty of each one of us to protect and preserve the beauty and fragrance of this one world flower from being destroyed?"

Success is everyone's most favorite mantra in today's world. In fact, what people are seeking in life has always been the same. It's only the words and interpretations that change.

Different cultures define success differently. For most people it is money, power, and pleasure similar to a Hedonistic philosophy. As Siduri, a character in the *Epic of Gilgamesh* (an epic poem from Mesopotamia) advises, "Fill your belly. Day and night make merry. Let days be full of joy. Dance and make music day and night. These things alone are the concern of men." Subsequently, other versions of hedonisms such as ethical hedonism, Christian hedonism, utilitarianism, Epicureanism, and so forth came into being.

India had Charvaka, a Heterodox Hindu, who advocated a materialistic philosophy. His view was, "Once the body turns into ashes, there is no coming back; therefore eat, drink, indulge, and be merry." Although they differ in names, fundamentally these approaches are all based in materialism, a pleasure seeking life. The difference is only in degree. In today's world, except for a marginal minority, the vast majority is rooted in a similar philosophy. All our definitions and concepts of success in all areas of activity and life can ultimately be summarized as materialistic.

We think our lives are very long, but Amma says that, in fact, they are very short. It's like a bubble compared to infinite time. Life is like a large sack of gold given to us at birth—a wonderful present. But as soon as we take our first breath, the universe starts collecting the time. And it doesn't stop—ever. It keeps on taking and taking and taking until we are bankrupt. And when we're bankrupt, we get a visit from Death. So live life to the fullest.

Recently I read an editorial in one of the mainstream news-papers. The writer, a well-known management consultant, said, "Greed in itself is good, as it gives people a reason to wake up in the morning and go to work and try to succeed at something. It is when people cross the line and move from doing something good to something unethical and criminal that the notion of greed turns bad."

Khaled Hosseini, currently a Goodwill Envoy for the United Nations High Commissioner for Refugees (UNHCR), writes in his novel, 'The Kite Runner,' a NY Times bestseller, "That same night, I wrote my first short story. It took me thirty minutes. It was a dark little tale about a man who found a magic cup and learned that if he wept into the cup, his tears turned into pearls. But even though he had always been poor, he was a happy man and rarely shed a tear. So he found ways to make himself sad so that his tears could make him rich. As the pearls piled up, his greed magnified. The story ended with the man sitting on a mountain of pearls, knife in hand, weeping helplessly into the cup with his beloved wife's slain body in his arms."

Having read the synopsis of this story, I imagine you agree with me that the assessment in the editorial ("Greed in itself is good") is not appropriate. Regardless of the resulting response, the driving force shouldn't be greed. Rather, it should be a deep feeling of joy regarding what we are doing. We should have a broader purpose than the accumulation of wealth.

Amma says, "To desire is natural to human beings. It's part of existence. But greed and intense craving are unnatural and are against existence, against God. The same is applicable to wasting food and taking more than you need from nature. These actions are opposed to the laws set by nature."

How do you explain recession in one simple sentence? It is corporate greed flooding throughout society. The crux of which is that we consciously or unconsciously forget the internal wealth of contentment. We don't care to develop the inner knowledge of discrimination.

Just a few years back, prized possessions such as a car, a cell phone, etc. were seen as luxuries. Now they are necessities. So, luxuries of the past have become necessities of today. Necessities are now being manifested as an increase in desire. It doesn't stop there. These desires are now taking the evil form of extreme greed and exploitation. This attitude has resulted in a loss of fundamental values, which in turn is causing an imbalance in resources. Even when we see the world around us falling apart, we don't want to change our mentality. We continue to exploit.

'Wants are unlimited!' according to economists. In life, too, wants or desires are important goals to fulfill.

"While contemplating the objects of the senses, a person develops attachment for them, and from such attachment desire

develops, and when any impediment comes in the path of enjoying that desire, a force called anger manifests itself. From anger, delusion arises, and from delusion bewilderment of memory. When memory is bewildered, intelligence is lost, and when intelligence is lost, one falls down from one's position."

—Bhagavad Gita, Chapter 2, Verses 62 – 63

If the disease that has caught hold of a person becomes the very essence of that person, he or she will not realize that there is a disease. When such ignorance turns to be the substance of our existence, there is no way out.

The real key to success is forgetting the past and being in the present, in the moment.

Amma says, "Living in the present doesn't mean we should not plan. While drawing the plan of a bridge, be completely there. And while building the bridge, be fully present there. When a doctor is operating on a patient, he should not be thinking about his wife and children at home. If he doesn't remain perfectly focused in the moment, he may lose the patient right on the operating table. But when he is at home with his wife and children, he should be a good husband and father (or a female surgeon should be a good wife and mother). Carrying the office to home and home to work are both dangerous. Work becomes joyful only when we are able to infuse love into it. Love is in the present. So, falling in love with our work is the same as reconnecting with the very source of happiness. In fact, it is not falling in love. If taken in the right spirit, it will help us rise in love and happiness. Preserve that joy, the deep feeling of love. It will gradually raise us to the level of a real master in our area of work."

In actuality, we forget our name, position, address, family, and status when we are totally absorbed in doing something that is of interest to us. It happens to poets, painters, singers, dancers, scientists, and people who contemplate on innovative ideas. That joyous mood comes from within. The source is not outside. In that state, we even become oblivious to the kind of work we are doing, whether it is a decent job or menial labor, because enjoyment becomes more important.

Years ago, when the headquarters of the MAM in Kerala was nothing but a small piece of land surrounded by backwaters, one of the regular routines of the residents was 'Sand Seva.' This was a service opportunity for everyone to help fill the swampy areas around the Center with new sand. The sand ferried from distant places would be piled on the banks of the backwaters. From there it would be shoveled into baskets, which would then be carried on peoples' heads to the respective filling grounds.

After the evening prayers and dinner, the sand seva bell would ring at any time. It had become so much part of the normal routine for the residents that everyone would be eagerly waiting to hear the sound of the bell. It could go at 10 o'clock, 11:00, 12:00, or even past midnight. As soon as the bell would ring, all the residents would be ready with baskets, shovels, spades, pickaxes, and other tools necessary for sand seva.

First, all the residents, irrespective of age, nationality, gender, and language would gather in front of Amma's room and wait for her. Soon Amma would come and say, "Okay, let us make a move…" Amma would be at the forefront participating fully. Sometimes she would scoop sand into sacks. At other times she would carry a sack of sand on her shoulders all the way to the swamp. Simultaneously, Amma would be overseeing the entire work and giving instructions. She would crack a joke every now and then, sing a song, and sometimes she would do a few dance steps with the sand on her head or shoulder. Even if the residents tried to stop her carrying the heavy sack of sand and using the shovel to scoop the sand, she would smilingly say, "If you can, I can, too."

Each member of the team would be working with utmost sincerity, enthusiasm, and love. It was fun, a truly joyous occasion, where work spontaneously transformed itself into playfulness, as if everyone was dancing. People were not even aware of the passing of time. The sand seva would normally last for a little over two hours. Finally the work would come to a halt when everyone heard Amma saying, "Enough for today." It would be long past midnight by then.

But that wasn't the end. Leading the entire group back to the NGO headquarters, Amma's next question would be, "Is the black coffee ready? Do you have the mixture and chips?" (A mixture is normally various fried items and salty banana chips.) As soon as the coffee and mixture arrived, Amma would sit in the sand surrounded by the residents. She would then serve the black coffee and mixture to everyone.

I vividly remember an incident that happened during one such occasion. As Amma was distributing coffee and chips to everyone, she suddenly said to one of the residents who was about to get his share of chips and coffee, "You haven't worked, have you?"

"No, I went to bed."

"Is it fair to enjoy the fruit of other people's action?" she asked in a calm voice.

"No." He replied honestly. "I am sorry, Amma." As he walked away, Amma called him back and said, "I don't want you to feel sad. It makes me also sad. But at the same time, I neither want others to feel upset with you, nor do I want to set a wrong example. I can't be partial. It should not create an impression in others that they can also get away with it. The mind is so sneaky that it is always looking for excuses to run away from situations and responsibilities. Am I wrong? What do you think?"

This time the resident seemed really apologetic. He said, "Amma, you are perfectly right." At that point Amma told him, "Now do one thing. Just carry one bag of sand from the banks of the backwaters to where we were filling the swamp and come back. You will get your share of coffee and chips." When he left to do as Amma instructed, she told others, "He has to carry one sack because Amma doesn't want to be unfair to those who have been working selflessly. Enjoyment and relaxation are an outcome of selfless action."

We may tend to think that Amma was too fussy by blowing a negligible mistake out of proportion and making it look like a serious transgression. However, our habits and character that shape our personality originate from thoughts that we normally brush aside as unsubstantial or immaterial. We all know how accumulation of instances of wrongdoings can escalate into dangerous situations. For example, thievery normally begins with insignificant or petty stealing and then escalates.

Often, success also starts small and grows. The genesis of several multinational corporations, including Microsoft and Apple, was modest. Two multinationals of India, Tata and Reliance, had humble beginnings as well. The initial capital investment at Infosys was only US$250. From there it has grown to a US$7.4

billion company with a market capitalization of approximately US$31 billion.

An apple falling down is not a big deal. However, in Sir Isaac Newton's mind it opened up an entire new world, which led to a great discovery. Everything in nature begins small. A huge tree springs forth from a tiny seed. According to the Big-Bang theory, the entire universe expanded from a small ball of singularity. As Ralph Ransom, the American painter said, "Life is a series of steps. Things are done gradually. Once in a while there is a giant step, but most of the time we are taking small, seemingly insignificant steps on the stairway of life."

Amma says, "There is nothing unsubstantial in this world, everything is substantial, everything is significant. An airplane cannot take off if its engine has a technical problem. Nor will the plane be able to take off if a vital screw is missing. Compared to the engine, the screw is small. Can we say that the engine is big whereas the screw is small, so let's not bother about it? No, we cannot."

As responsible citizens and contributors to society, it is important to understand that nothing can be discarded as unimportant. There is a purpose behind everything.

Readers should know that, in fact, almost the entire spiritual Center's premises that we see today in Kerala, India were once marshland. Without engaging any outside contractors, it was the residents and guests who filled and leveled the land to its existing condition, continually guided by Amma's physical presence and participation.

Although the sand seva incident narrated earlier seems to be small, it conveys the need to cultivate awareness in all circumstances of life. As Amma puts it, "Without awareness there is no life. True awareness is to be aware of the movements of the body, things that are happening outside the body, and the thoughts and emotions that occur in the mind. This indeed is the way to check the vices from dominating us." I am reminded of a saying by Aristotle, "The ultimate value of life depends upon awareness and the power of contemplation rather than upon mere survival."

The sand seva story also points to the call for an affectionate and humble attitude when approaching people and dealing with situations. Amma telling the resident, "I don't want you to feel sad. It makes me also sad," shows her affection for her team members. By not giving coffee and chips to the resident who didn't participate in the sand seva, Amma clearly sent the message of 'fair dealing' and 'You cannot always stick to your own ways—be a team player.' In this way, she made everyone happy.

The most worthwhile point is the way Amma transforms normal work into a joyful experience and demonstrates the capacity of a leader to truly inspire her team members and sustain their high spirits, regardless of the time of day or night. As J.R.D. Tata rightly observed, "When we want to win people, we have to win by character and kindness. To be a leader, you have got to lead human beings with affection."

Chapter Four

Virtuous and Vicious Cycles

The economic terms 'virtuous circle' and 'vicious circle' are also known as 'virtuous cycle' and 'vicious cycle.' The terms normally refer to a series of intricate occurrences that reinforce forward movement or favorable results through what might be called a feedback loop. As the terms suggest, a virtuous circle has encouraging results, whereas a vicious circle has discouraging or unfavorable results.

A virtuous circle might be created when innovations in science and technology cause growth in the economy. The chain reaction would be increased efficiency in production, reduced costs, lower prices, and higher buying power and consumption, which would cause even greater growth in the economy, thereby starting a new cycle. Another example might be compound interest earned on monies deposited, which keeps on generating greater amounts of interest and favorably influences increased monies being deposited, thus increasing the interest and so on.

Hyperinflation is a characteristic outcome of a vicious circle, which causes spiral inflation resulting in even higher inflation. This cycle normally begins with rapidly increasing international rates or enormous escalation in government arrears, mainly owing to unwarranted expenditures. The government may try to reduce the liabilities by minting more currency, otherwise known as monetizing the debt, but an augmented supply in money may further accelerate the intensity of inflation. Anticipating a future decline in the value of money, people will be inclined to spend their money quickly. Since money continues to have some purchasing power, people convert their financial savings into material assets. Quite often these purchases will be on credit, which ultimately zeros down the value of money. As the savings of the country decline, the government will find it difficult to pay back its liabilities, leaving minting more currency as the only escape route. This initiates yet another vicious cycle. Indian currency policy is different from western countries, mainly the United States and some of the European countries. The Reserve Bank of India (RBI) deposits a certain percentage of gold in their vaults, in proportion to monetization, thus minimizing the possibility of inflation.

Because we humans have failed to use available resources, both natural and otherwise, in a sensible manner, unless we take a drastic step to improve the current situation, a state of imbalance is bound to be the consequence. The widening gap between the rich and the poor will result in an unfair and unequal distribution of resources, which will automatically invite unhappiness, discontentment, and conflict.

It is time to incorporate new principles that may not appear intellectually compelling but are vital ingredients when viewed from the point where humanity is standing now. The improved approach would be to move from the calculative heart to the sensitive heart. It is time to create a certain degree of balance between decisions made using intelligence, pure reasoning, and logical analysis versus those made using the heart, conscience, and the power beyond so that our external and internal worlds move hand in hand.

The whispering of our conscience is soft, subtle, and subjective, so we also need to employ the skill of deep listening. Let us try to develop a habit of holding a tête-à-tête with our own conscience. If your conscience ever suggests or says "No" to something, don't proceed. We have been completely neglecting our conscience while engaged in exploiting our natural resources.

I have no doubt that most readers would agree with me that our planet earth badly needs our loving support and compassionate approach. The call is not something that can only be experienced by subtle and sensitive minds. It is so palpable. People all over the world, the animal and plant kingdoms, our rivers, the entire nature, and the atmosphere are exhibiting clear signs of an unforeseen tragedy. To be blunt, it is a 'do or die' situation. We have only two choices: Either make immediate internal and external changes, or we are free to stick to our old patterns and let nature take its own course of action.

I'm reminded of the words of Professor Stephen Hawking, the world's most famous astrophysicist. In an interview for Big Think idea hunters, he said, "I see great dangers for the human race. There have been a number of times in the past when its survival has been a question of touch and go. The Cuban missile crisis in 1963 was one of these. The frequency of such occasions is likely to increase in the future. We shall need great care and judgment to negotiate them all successfully. But I'm an optimist. If we can avoid disaster for the next two centuries, our species should be safe, as we spread into space.

"If we are the only intelligent beings in the galaxy, we should make sure we survive and continue. But we are entering an increasingly dangerous period of our history. Our population and our use of the finite resources of planet Earth are growing exponentially, along with our technical ability to change the environment for good or ill. But our genetic code still carries the selfish and aggressive instincts that were our survival advantage in the past. It will be difficult enough to avoid disaster in the next hundred years, let alone the next thousand or million. Our only chance of long-term survival is not to remain inward looking on planet Earth, but to spread out into space. We have made remarkable progress in the last hundred years. But if we want to continue beyond the next hundred years, our future is in space. That is why I'm in favor of manned, or should I say 'personed,' space flight."

Though Professor Hawking observed that "spreading out into space" is "our only chance of long term survival," from a practical point of view, this may not be possible. But, if man wills, with the help of the law that governs the universe, we can still transform this planet Earth into a resourceful and beautiful place for generations to come. This change demands a metamorphosis that is all about experiencing, expressing, and practicing love, the most endearing emotion for humanity and all other living beings. Or, we can shut our eyes to everything that happens in the world, focus on our own immediate satisfactions, and say, "Let me not be bothered about the world and the generations to come." Before adhering to that attitude, imagine the condition of our world if every individual were to think along those lines.

In fact, 'Love is a medium.' As a medium, it connects human beings with the universe, mother with child (no matter whether it is a human child, an animal's, or a bird's fledgling). It is the link that connects every one of us with the other, but this inherent love has to be nourished. Perhaps, love is not the 'space' that Hawking refers to. But in reality, love has always been man's 'space', humanity's true unexplored abode. Love will continue to be our real 'space' of existence in the present and future as well, unless we choose to exit from that sacred space. The crux of Amma's brand as the Ambassador of the Mirror Model is 'Take Birth in Love, Live in Love, and Die in Love.'

Just one word is sufficient to describe Amma's compassionate nature: *Giving*. The massive humanitarian activities she has initiated and the contributions she had made in the areas of education, healthcare, research, empowering women, building homes for the homeless, environmental protection, free meals, etc. can be summed up in this one word. Speaking on Amma's accomplishment in this regard, Dr. A.P.J. Abdul Kalam, the former President of India, offered this testimony, "I want to share with you what I have learned from Amma: Giving. Go on giving. It's not only money. You can share knowledge. You can remove the pain. Every one of us—the rich and poor—can give. There is no greater message than Amma's giving to all the people of the world."

Amma is a visionary, but one who has also clearly demonstrated the capacity to deliver. As the mayor of New York City, Michael Bloomberg, said, "From providing tsunami relief to building homes for the poor, to providing valuable resources to widows and abused women, to simply providing comfort to those who need it most, Amma, you have made a difference for so many grateful men and women all across the globe."

As Krishna stated in the *Bhagavad Gita*: *yogah karmasu kausalam*—"Yoga is dexterity in action." Amma thinks, decides, and acts with amazing speed. With each project, Amma selflessly takes initiative, focuses on her duty, and doesn't worry about the outcomes or the results.

Here are some of her projects:

HUMANITARIAN AID

Disaster Relief—

- LPG Tanker & Fireworks Factory Explosions in South India (2012): aid to families of dead and injured
- Japan Earthquake/Tsunami (2011): $1 million U.S., focus on children orphaned in the disaster
- Haiti Earthquake (2010): Medical supplies, blankets, providing scholarships to students
- Floods in Karnataka & Andhra Pradesh (2009): $10.7 million relief package including medical care, food, supplies and 1,000 homes for displaced refugees
- Cyclone Aila, West Bengal, (2009): Medical care, food and supplies
- Floods in Bihar (2008), Gujarat (2006), Mumbai (2005): Over S1.5 mil. in medical, food, supplies and shelter
- Earthquake, Kashmir (2005): Food and supplies
- Hurricane Katrina, USA (2005): $1 million U.S. to Bush-Clinton Katrina Fund
- Tsunami, India and Sri Lanka (2004): Provided a value of $46 million in relief (built 6,200 tsunami-resistant homes, 700 new fishing boats and an evacuation bridge, provided vocational training for 2,500 victims).
- Earthquake, Gujarat (2001): 1,200 earthquake-resistant homes

Other Aid Projects—

- Completion of 45,000 homes for the poor throughout India
- Providing 41,000 scholarships for children of impoverished farmers, with a goal of 100,000

- Empowering 100,000 women by providing start-up capital, vocational ed. and access to microcredit loan
- Organic Farming Initiative supporting 10,000 poor people to grow organic vegetables on their own land.
- Orphanages for 500 children in Kerala and 50 children in Nairobi
- Yearly feeding over 10 milllion poor inside India and 100,000 outside, including 75,000 in USA via soup kitchens
- Pensions for 59,000 destitute women and the physically and mentally challenged, with goal of 100,000
- Four care-homes for the elderly in India
- Hostel providing secure housing for women
- Prisoner-welfare project in U.S. provides solace for prison inmates

Spiritual, Cultural—

- Amritapuri Ashram (Kerala, India) is the international headquarters for Amma's service work, which is carried out through hundreds of branch centers and service groups world-wide
- IAM® Technique (Integrated Amrita Meditation Technique®) taught free throughout the world
- AYUDH helps youth "Be the change you wish to see in the world" via community-outreach projects
- GreenFriends cultivates reverence for Nature and has arranged and inspired planting 1 mil. trees since 2001

Healthcare—

Amrita Institute of Medical Sciences (AIMS)

- Not-for-profit 1,300-bed hospital (210-bed ICU) provides free care to the poor
- 12 main specialty institutes, 51 associated medical departments, 24 operating theatres
- More than 2.6 million patients have received completely free treatment since 1998

AIMS Community Service

- Telemedicine for hospitals and more than 40 remote centers across India and in parts of Africa
- Free health screenings in remote areas providing preventative healthcare
- Training of hundreds of tribal villagers as healthcare workers
- Five branch hospitals (three in Kerala, one in Karnataka and one in Andaman Island) provide free care
- AIDS care-home in Trivandrum and cancer hospice in Mumbai
- Free palliative in-home care for the terminally ill
- More than 100 free medical camps annually throughout India
- Ayurvedic medicine through the School of Ayurveda's 160-bed hospital
- Providing 100,000 women with training to become in-home nurses in more than 6,000 self-help groups

Education—

Amrita Vishwa Vidyapeetham (Amrita University)
- Five campuses with Schools of Engineering, Medicine, Nursing, Dentistry, Pharmacy, Business, Journalism, Ayurveda, Education, Biotechnology and Arts & Sciences
- Amrita Research Labs and other Research Departments are continuously developing innovations in communication, e-learning, educational technologies, computer sciences and biotechnology
- 30 leading universities worldwide, including Stanford, MIT, NYU, EPFL in Switzerland, VU in Amsterdam, TU Munich, Roma Tre, ETH Zurich and the University of Tokyo cooperate with Amrita University to enhance higher education and research in India
- Institute of Peoples' Education provides job-training and community development
- United Nations commended literacy-training program for tribal populations

Elementary and Secondary Education
- 47 schools throughout India with a values-based, holistic approach to learning
- A school for hearing-impaired children in Kerala

Amma's whole effort is to create a virtuous circle, thereby blocking the possibility of being drawn into the whirlpool of a vicious circle, which spreads the germs of negativity to everyone like a contagious disease.

Chapter Five

Virtue, Equanimity, and Grace

As explained in the previous chapter, economists have their own way of describing virtuous and vicious circles. Amma's leadership and management produces an extraordinary love-based virtuous circle that constantly produces and shapes goodhearted human beings.

When one bad thing leads to another, we call it a vicious circle. Take fear for example. When we are in the grip of fear, if not overcome, the fear leads to increased fear, which will eventually trigger more and more fear. Thus, we get into a vicious circle. With each incident of fear, the emotion will move deeper and deeper into our mind. The more we allow fear to control us, the fear becomes more deeply imbedded and develops into a habit, affecting our words, our energy, and our demeanor.

Contrary to this, in a virtuous circle such as Amma develops, because the leader walks the walk and talks the talk, people feel tremendously inspired by her fairness, love for humanity, power, patience to listen, fearlessness, etc. When such a powerful living example heads the organization, the team will have a natural urge to emulate the positive characteristics. This connection and the cycle it creates becomes a catalyst that allows the organization to accomplish astonishing results.

An example of Amma's equal vision and caring attitude comes to mind: After our NGO finished the tsunami relief and rehabilitation activities, we wanted to create a document for future use and reference by putting all of the details in book form. When the sample copy of the book was ready, we showed it to Amma before sending it to the printing press. It was quite a large book filled with photos and vivid descriptions. While giving darshan, Amma flipped through the pages and looked at all the photographs of the various tsunami-relief seva projects. There were pictures of Amma working alongside the volunteers, senior monks, residents, westerners, young and old alike, engaged in various seva activities. We even had a picture of Ram, one of the ashram elephants, carrying wood as part of the house-construction work. While glancing through the picture book, Amma all of a sudden shouted, "Where is Lakshmi?" At first I didn't understand. I thought Amma was referring to Lakshmi, Amma's personal attendant. But Amma said, "No, Lakshmi! Lakshmi! Lakshmi," she explained, "It is not fair. You have pictures of Raman but not Lakshmi. She also did tsunami work." Amma was referring to the second ashram elephant, Lakshmi. This is real fairness, not just for human beings but also for the animals.

Amma's example of selflessness and caring attracts brilliant scientists, physicians, and professionals from throughout the world and integrates them into the university or the healthcare facilities as she carefully manages resources and circumstances. This type of leadership spontaneously creates a virtuous circle.

For Amma, her entire life, even today, is filled with trials and tribulations. Initially it was her family and the villagers. Though they have completely accepted her now, from the age of nine, when she stopped going to school, until the late 1980's, Amma had to face and surmount countless obstacles. No one in her family or in the village had any understanding of the path of love and compassion she pursued. Particularly, Amma being a young girl, family members were greatly concerned about her future. But her faith and commitment to lead a life of compassion and care was unshakably firm.

Amma has fashioned a vast network of virtuous circles starting from small children to grown ups from all walks of life. Thus, Amma is initiating a process of purification and commitment even in small children, creating a worldwide phenomenon where children associated with Amma's organization set aside money they receive from relatives to support charitable activities.

A couple of years ago, when Amma was in Switzerland, a boy around thirteen years old approached her with a small envelope in his hands. Handing it over to Amma, the boy said, "This is for your charitable activities."

Amma enquired, "What is in it?"

"Three hundred euros," replied the boy.

"Where did it you get it from?" Amma asked.

"I participated in a flute-performance competition and won first prize. This is the prize money. You do so much to help the poor. Please accept this." The boy's words were filled with untainted love and innocence. Amma insisted that he should keep the money for his personal use.

But the story did not end there.

The boy's little sister felt sad because she couldn't offer anything to help the poor. But then, a few weeks later, it was her birthday. Amma was in Munich at that time. The little girl's grandfather gave her a small amount as a birthday gift. Normally she would buy ice cream or chocolates with the money he gave her, but this time, after receiving the pocket money, the girl told her parents, "I eat ice cream all the time. But this time I want to give the money to my Amma. She takes care of so many children like me, doesn't she?"

This is how purification of love occurs. It happens through association, understanding, and a genuine concern for others. The boy and the girl still had a desire, a desire to serve less fortunate children.

An inspiring example can definitely reach out and touch every heart. Such a role model crosses language, country, religion, and age and helps people to gradually have pure goals and intentions. This is how Amma helps people to unfold their hearts.

Just as with any other undertaking, the path of virtue demands unwavering faith and fortitude. As one's staying power deepens, things gradually change. One's work, thoughts, and presence gain a natural acceptance and respect. At the same time, an individual following this path will be a mystery, because calculative minds will find it difficult to understand the power of virtue that, when translated into action, becomes a way of life. Once we enter the circle of virtue, our inner power and potential flourish. Virtue protects us from all odds because we are now connected with the eternal law of the universe. We become one with that flow.

The circle of virtue also allows us to become more centered, regardless of external circumstances. We thoroughly enjoy our external successes, but when an external failure happens, we remain centered in the experience of our inner virtue. This inner centeredness is just a question of awareness.

The greatest advantage of entering into the virtuous circle is that it completely blocks the unnecessary meddling of the ego. The normal belief all over the world is that nothing can be achieved without the ego. Nevertheless, the truth is that the ego is not a real friend, rather a foe, a stumbling block that prevents us from seeing, listening, observing, and judging things properly. It's like a humongous cloud that envelops the entire expansive sky of our mind, thus obscuring reality. By minimizing the intervention of the ego, our mental clarity, brilliance, efficiency, and proficiency take a big leap. This checking of the ego allows our decisions to be made more quickly and precisely.

The more we minimize the interference of the ego, the greater the support and protection we receive from the universe. It is almost like some unknown power carrying us through the various challenges of life. In fact, at this point, the law of grace, the law that governs the universe, becomes activated in our everyday life.

The law of grace initiates a process of vertical as well as horizontal growth. We develop a special faculty to turn every barrier into a blessing, yet another rung to step on and ascend to the next level of victory. However, this reversal doesn't mean that problems will disappear and situations will undergo a dramatic change. Don't expect the external situations to change, but there will definitely be a shift in our inner world.

Grace is an 'unknown phenomenon' that comes from a place that is incomprehensible to us. For the successful completion of a project, we need this aspect called Grace. For example, we may have a vision, but we may not have the Grace to bring that vision to reality. John F. Kennedy laid out his vision of landing a human being on the moon and bringing him back safely to earth on May 25, 1961. Kennedy knew that there was tremendous competition with other nations in the field of space research. He wanted the United Sates to be the first country to put a man on the moon. However, his vision did not take place during his tenure as President of the United States. It happened only in 1969 when Mr. Richard Nixon was the President.

John F. Kennedy might have been a more popular President of the United States. However, something behind the curtains, an invisible power, decided that the credit of sending a human being to the moon and bringing him back to earth safely should go to President Richard Nixon. There are so many other such examples in the history of humanity. Instances keep happening and shall continue to do so.

The earth, through its gravitational force, attracts and causes everything to fall down. This we consider as a universal law. No one can deny the fact that in life everything has a dual nature: happiness and sorrow, success and failure, gain and loss, honor and dishonor, summer and winter, rain and shine, etc. In a similar manner, in order to balance the external law of gravitation, which draws everything downwards, there must be an internal law that helps us to soar and rise above all situations. That is the law of grace. Amma explains, "As long as the weight of the ego weighs us down, the wind of grace cannot carry us up."

While a vicious circle is connected with the lower emotions, a virtuous circle is connected to a higher level of consciousness. Amma helps people to shift their consciousness from the lower to the higher, thus forming a worldwide circular chain of virtuous people.

Chapter Six

Small Corrections, Big Changes

There is a beautiful saying by Aristotle: "Anybody can become angry — that is easy; but to be angry with the right person, and to the right degree, and at the right time, and for the right purpose, and in the right way, that is not within everyone's power and is not easy."

In a money-focused and results-oriented society with intense cravings and inexhaustible desiring as its hallmark, it is understandable if people don't take Aristotle seriously. Even so, an intelligent and contemplative person cannot deny the philosophical depth, physiological insight, and the gem of a great spiritual truth that is hidden in the words. Anyone capable of absorbing the meaning of these words by translating them into action will experience a glorious change in their life.

In many countries and cultures, theoretical and practical management systems are undergoing a change. It is high time that this transformation should happen, or else the physically, emotionally, and intellectually overburdened members of the corporate world will face a nervous breakdown. Many business people complain that their life has become mechanical and monotonous, that the spontaneity is gone, that there is no joy or playfulness.

As I see it, the nitty-gritty of Aristotle's saying can be summarized in three words: Awareness, Witnessing, and Listening. The last two, witnessing and listening, depend on our level of awareness. Don't think that I am putting across a suggestion that the readers should become extreme practitioners of these qualities. Even a fair amount of practice can bring vast benefits.

There is a verse in the *Bhagavad Gita*, where Krishna tells Arjuna,

> *Svalpam Apyasya Dharmasya Trayate*
> *Mahato Bhayat...*
>
> *A little practice of spiritual truths can help you cross over the biggest of fears.*

We accumulate and try to assimilate a great deal of self-help information from websites, blogs, online newspapers, books, magazines, and various other sources. What is the use of all this information if it doesn't provide us with a solid substratum where we can more steadily position ourselves to face the challenges of life with inner strength, understanding, and depth?

It isn't just information that we accumulate. There are people who go on collecting anything and everything they find. It is a deep-rooted habit of hoarding. They may collect the old, discarded parts of a motorbike from the dumping grounds. One handle, a seat, one broken wheel, a pedal, a useless indicator light, and yet another handle of some other motorbike manufactured by a different company. They keep gathering all this waste and fill their only room. If somebody asks them, "Why do you collect all this trash?" they would say, "I am going to put all these parts together one day and make a motorbike for myself." It never happens, and the man may die without ever fulfilling 'the castle he has been building in the air.'

What I mean to say is that the mere collection of information without putting it into practice will only serve to increase the load, draining our mental capacities and blocking our clarity of vision and thinking.

Aristotle's words illuminate a clear path to success, fame, and power. His advice, "Be angry with the right person, to the right degree, at the right time, for the right purpose, and in the right way…" Should not all leaders, managers, and CEO's strive to develop this capability?

One should be aware though that this advice demands a witnessing attitude, the skill to detach oneself from the project at hand and look at it from the perspective of an observer. Once we learn this invaluable skill, we see many unseen and important aspects of the world around us. It is like removing the lid of a trunk holding a hidden treasure or unwrapping a priceless gift. In the Indian scriptures, this attitude of witnessing is described as 'Sakshi Bhava.' It is almost like consciously lifting yourself to an astral plane for some time. So basically, it raises your consciousness level from where you get a better view of everything you do and all that is going on around you.

With regard to listening, it is not just hearing what other people say but also listening to our own conscience. Our conscience never lies. So, listening to it will invariably help us make better decisions.

The Indian scriptures say, 'Listen, Reflect and Practice.' The first step is external listening. If you are reading a book or listening to a lecture, don't even write notes. Just listen, drink in every word. The second step, reflection, is internal listening. Use your reasoning faculty for a deep inquiry into that which you have heard. This discipline leads to a genuine experience of the subject of study followed by true internalization of it. A sincere pursuit of this path opens up the sixth sense, the intuitive mind. A seeker of truth can go further beyond and merge into the state of pure bliss.

Albert Einstein says, "The intuitive mind is a sacred gift, and the rational mind is a faithful servant. We have created a society that honors the servant and has forgotten the gift."

Because our awareness level is low, we remain identified with the objective world, completely forgetting the subjective world. So, when something goes wrong outside, our mind 'goes wrong.' When the stock market collapses, we collapse. When failure happens, an internal failure takes place. This affects our life and our entire thinking process. We are too close, too identified with the problem, and we fail to see the big picture. We lose our clarity and discrimination.

In order to get a well-defined vision of the scenario, we have to step outside the problem and view it from a distance. As an example, hold your palms close to your eyes and try to see the palm lines. None of the lines will be distinct. Now hold them 18 inches away—we see all the lines clearly. Similar is the case with a situation and people. Just as we adjust and reposition our hand to see all the lines and marks on our palm, it is necessary to make certain mental adjustments, a tuning, which brings out all the details and provides a deeper insight into the matter. On the other hand, when we are too identified with our ideas and strategies, we miss the broader picture. Detachment will help us effectively face and intelligently handle the diverse challenges that life brings.

Amma gives an example, "Suppose a close relative of your neighbor dies. We go there, console the family and even quote from the scriptures that 'Death is inevitable.' Because we are a witness to this situation, we don't identify with the problem, and therefore we are able to keep a distance from it. But when one of our close family members dies, we are unable to practice what we preached as we are too close to the problem; we become one with it. We lose our emotional center. We must find a way to stay balanced and detached."

We cannot change a situation, change another person, control the future or obtain full satisfaction and security from anything external. The only option available is to gain proficiency in utilizing the inner world to rise above the situation and see it from a higher level of consciousness. This is the sum and substance of the teaching of the Bhagavad Gita. I wonder if this was what Peter Drucker meant when he said, "One cannot manage change. One can only be ahead of it."

Take the example of an Indian high school student who has his heart set on becoming a doctor. There is a great deal of pressure to meet the expectations of his parents. Exams in the 12th grade determine this child's entire future. Depending on the scores, one will go on to medical school, engineering, business school or maybe another career path that doesn't involve studying at a university. Everyone is so focused on the goal of doing well in this exam that disappointment is inevitable. Yet, preparing for the exam is within the student's control, but the outcome is not. Nevertheless, every single student appearing for the 12th grade exam and every parent across the country is under immense pressure during this period. It is real suffering.

Instead of feeling pressured by the fear, anxiety, and stress of worrying about the result of the exam, is it not just common sense to focus on what is controllable rather than what is not? Action is in the present. We should pay full attention to this action. That alone is under our control. The future is beyond our power. This is such a simple truth.

When the parent helps the child to understand this, doesn't it take away the heavy burden of tension? Doesn't it help both the parent and child to channel more energy to the task at hand in order to teach and study well? When the parent and child are not attached to the outcome and they accept the unpredictable future, things just flow. While engaged in performing an action, forget the result if you can. It will lift the burden from your shoulders and keep you relaxed and focused.

Regardless of your area of activity or what you are trying to accomplish, the practice of witnessing (the art of non-attachment) is beneficial. It will enhance your company's productivity and improve your managerial skills. Encourage your employees to practice this technique as well. G.K. Chesterton said, "Angels fly because they take themselves lightly." To become lighter to soar to new heights, reduce the weight of the ego, the burden of unnecessary attachment.

Let's consider a situation where there may be a conflict. I learned about the value of "witnessing" the world around me from Amma years ago. I now understand that we are in the audience observing an incredible and complex drama of human life. Occasionally, we may wander onto the stage, but for the most part, our role is to stay in our seat and watch what is going on. When we assume this aerial view, we are able to see all vantage points, to consider all perspectives, to truly think globally.

Once I heard Amma say, "If one wants to save a drowning person, they have to keep a safe distance while pulling him or her out of the water, holding onto their hair. Otherwise, the drowning person will pull the one who is trying to save them into deep waters as well. Both will drown."

When we are detached from the outcome, the probability of achieving the goal increases. In a similar manner, developing a certain degree of non-attachment while discharging our duties in the world will help us to remain alert and aware in all circumstances. To quote Amma, "A bird perched on a dry twig may chirp, eat, or even sleep, but it will be ready to take flight at any moment. With even the slightest wind, its wings will flutter in preparation for flight because it knows that the dry twig could snap and break at any moment."

I think a story about witnessing might be helpful here. A French director, Jan Kounen, made a documentary film on Amma, 'Darshan—The Embrace.' The movie officially showcased at the 2004 Cannes Film Festival. The screening in Cannes was on May 18th of that year. They really wanted Amma to be present, but she did not want to cancel her already scheduled programs, so she politely turned down their request. Instead, Amma asked me to represent her. So I went to Cannes as Amma's emissary.

During my stay there, I had to mingle and interact with many people from the entertainment industry. While interacting with my new friends from the film fraternity world and attending several parties, two in luxury yachts and others in five star hotels, I still maintained my witness perspective.

When I returned, people were curious. Many people asked, "Come on, how did it feel walking the red carpet and being there?" Of course, as a *sanyasi* (monk), they thought it was strange for me to be there. But I told them, "I was only a messenger. I was there. I participated. It was a responsibility entrusted to me by Amma, my boss. And I had to perform it with all sincerity and love. So, I did it. But, since I was fully aware of my 'emissary role,' I could remain as a spectator throughout the time I was there."

When you are asked to play the part, you have to do your best, without identifying with the role. I also had to give a short three-minute speech on Amma and her humanitarian activities to a large audience who had no previous exposure to Amma. And I had no idea about their spiritual inclinations.

Perhaps, that was the first time ever, in the history of the Cannes Film Festival, when a Hindu monk was there for the screening of a movie and representing the 'heroine!' There were people from all over the world. And most of them were either from the movie industry, were aficionados of movies, or were there to see the movie stars. I was in a predicament. I thought to myself, "How do I present Amma in the proper way? Speaking on love for God, self-surrender, etc. was out of the question. How could I help the audience to relate, to make the connection?"

My biggest fear was that the moment the audience saw a monk in orange clothes representing the 'heroine,' they would become judgmental and remain closed to the entire movie. Certainly, that could have happened if one was not careful. I closed my eyes for a few moments in a contemplative mood. Suddenly something dawned on me. During my school and college days, I had always wanted to become an actor and a musician. To be honest, those were the priorities in my life. I stood before the fully packed hall and said, "Dear brothers and sisters, twenty-six years ago, before becoming a monk, my life's goal was to become an actor. But, something happened, which brought me to my preceptor, Sri Mata Amritanandamayi Devi - Amma as she is known to the world."

The moment I uttered these words, the connection took place. The crowd laughed and applauded. That gave me confidence, and I continued, "It gives me great pleasure to stand here in front of you, such highly creative minds, and to be representing Amma. Friends, through your art, you have the ability to greatly influence and change people all over the world. Amma, too, transforms people's lives through her simple, yet profound, acts of love and compassion." Here, it wasn't logical thinking or analysis that I needed. It was the contemplation, non-attachment, emissary role that helped me.

The screening went well. We had a full house. And I think people liked the movie. To be an actor was my life's dream before meeting Amma. Regardless, I was neither elated by the crowd's response, nor regretful that my life path did not involve acting. I believe that the path I ultimately chose, or was bestowed upon me, is superior to any other path. Yet, here was a long cherished intense desire of mine coming true for a short period of time. To be part of the Cannes Film Festival is a great honor, a memorable moment for anyone in the movie industry. It is one of their dreams. Suppose the transformation that brought me to my current path had not occurred, I would have been immensely excited and considered this to be a momentous occasion in my life. I might have even gotten carried away. However, for me, something changed within; the inner world changed. Now I was only a messenger to fulfill a particular mission.

Extreme emotional states put our success at risk. So, it is important to mentally keep a distance. It is the capacity to step aside and watch the new experiences that helped me go through the parties and festival in a calm, composed, and relaxed manner, producing the right responses. Above all, even though I was in a world of people whose topic of discussion had no connection with my present life, I was still able to perform well by using my inner potential to the maximum.

Perhaps the experience was a design of the power beyond to exhaust any deep-seated karmic residue that remained within me so that my forward journey would be smoother. The most significant point is that the change in my perception made it easier for me to see the whole thing in a positive light, and success followed.

The messenger attitude gives us the inner capacity to view things from a safe distance, which, in turn, enables us to get a better understanding of the situation. It enhances precision and vision and thereby augments our performance level. As this inner ability attains greater depths, we acquire a new strength to overcome our lower emotions. We become the master, and our mind and our emotions become our servant. The tempting outside circumstances fail to influence us. As a leader, we gain more vitality, stability, and clarity of vision. The power to adjust and adapt with all sorts of situations and experiences increases tremendously. Similarly, when we remain unperturbed in the face of all odds, thinking, decision-making, and execution improves. This witness stance automatically increases our success.

One point that needs special mention is Amma's tremendous inner capacity to impartially view and evaluate any situation with an attitude of non-attachment. Most people think detachment is unhealthy. Those who lead a normal life feel that attachment is what makes life enjoyable, even though it rarely generates happiness. Conversely, it is Amma's subjective ability to instantly switch roles and the speed and ease with which she moves from one role to another is what makes Amma's personality so powerful, attractive, and inspiring. In that process of switching roles,

Amma completely forgets the previous moment, the role she had assumed just before, and remains completely focused on the one at hand. Nothing affects her calm and composed nature as she interacts with and gives instructions to her team members. In any circumstance you cannot see Amma viewing a situation or person with a judgmental attitude. Even when you see her being strict, that particular emotion or mood doesn't affect her inner being, and she moves out of it with absolute ease and dexterity. Her decisions come quickly, and when it comes to execution, her follow up is meticulous to the core.

Chapter Seven

Needle and Scissors

In an article that appeared in *Mail Online*, Amanda Williams writes, "'Great leaders are born, not made. Their brains are just wired differently,' scientists say."

The article goes on to say, "Research by a leading military academic claims to have put the debate to bed on whether it is nature or nurture which creates greatness after finding [that] the most effective really are a breed apart and have brains that are wired differently to most. The discovery could revolutionize how organizations assess and develop leaders, with brain scans being used to identify those with the 'leadership gene' early and [to] train them accordingly. It seems [that] the most successful have more grey matter in places that control decision-making and memory, giving them a vital edge when it comes to making the right call. Some people are, indeed, born leaders. These folks at the top of the leadership bell curve start out very good and tend to get even better as they go along. Then there are the folks at the bottom of the curve: that bottom 10-15% of people who, no matter how hard they try, simply aren't ever going to be very good leaders. They just don't have the innate wiring. Then there's the big middle of the curve, where the vast majority of us live. And that's where the real potential for "made" leaders lies. It's what most of my interviewers assume isn't true—when, in fact, it is: Most folks who start out with a modicum of innate leadership capability can actually become very good, even great leaders."

By way of explanation, a bell curve—a distinct bell shaped curve—refers to a 'Gaussian Distribution' or normal distribution. Compared to the upper and lower parts, the curve is more evident with more area in the middle, which makes it look like a bell. Professional courses are said to be "marked on the curve," meaning students bagging A+ will be only a small percentage. They are at the top of the curve. Grade A, next on the curve, will show a slight increase in percentage. The bulk, scoring grade C, belong to the middle portion of the bell curve. Sadly enough, a certain percentage, however, is bound to face the misfortune of failure. They fall on the bottom-most portion of the bell with an F grade. When illustrated with the help of a diagram, this entire structure will take a well-defined bell shape.

While debating the efficacy of born leaders versus self-made leaders, it would be unfair to forget a third category known as divine leaders. Even after thousands of years, this rare and phenomenal class of leaders are remembered, admired and worshipped by millions of people across the world. The eminence of this group of leaders is incomprehensive. Such is the power, the influence, and the impression that they have left in the hearts of humanity. We can only marvel looking at their inspiring and transforming presence, their indescribable work, their unconditional love and compassion for all of humanity and other forms of life, as well as the power of their words and the magnetism of their being. They are cherished and remembered as heroes, heroines, and perfect role models in all areas of life.

The massive number of followers and fans that these divine leaders have is unparalleled. No political party leaders, no celebrity, no other famous human being in the past, present, or in the future has such a following.

Amma says, "Intellect or logic is like a pair of scissors and the heart is like a needle. The intellect cuts everything into pieces, and the heart sews everything together. It is not enough to cut a fabric to size. We should also sew the pieces together and make clothing out of it, so that we can wear it. In fact, we need both intellect and the heart: the intellect to think and the heart to put the thoughts in a cohesive manner. Together they will cover and protect our life. Otherwise, our life will remain in pieces, useful, but equally harmful."

Being predominantly logical and analytical, we find it difficult to understand a leader of Amma's caliber. We forget the truth that life itself is not logical in nature.

It seems that our world is in the clutches of "The Centipede Syndrome." The following short poem beautifully depicts humanity's state:

A centipede was happy – quite!
Until a toad in fun
Said, "Pray, which leg moves after which?"
This raised her doubts to such a pitch,
She fell exhausted in the ditch
Not knowing how to run.

The author of this version of the poem is anonymous. However, there is a similar *Aesop's Fable*, where the toad is replaced with a rabbit. Referring to the poem, George Humphrey (1889–1966), the English psychologist, said, "This is a most psychological rhyme. It contains a profound truth which is illustrated daily in the lives of all of us."

Whoever you are, whatever you are doing, it is foolish to depend solely on intellect and logic alone to unfold life. Logic has its place, so does the unknown. An intellectually centered person with a strong inclination to analyze everything logically will not be able to help someone who is in such a tragic situation as the centipede. A deeper enquiry into the poem reveals that we human beings are also in a similar quandary. The only difference is that we don't need another person to ask the question. Our own mind will offer the questions and answers to create a monologue all by itself! The problem is that most of the time the mind doesn't know the right questions to ask so the answers are bound to be wrong, thus derailing our forward movement.

We definitely need rules to organize our lives in an orderly fashion and to control our day-to-day activities. We should also understand that life itself is not entirely calculative or mathematical. The mind has two compartments: one mechanical and the other natural. In other words, one part acts like a machine and the other is spontaneous. Therefore, we need to give equal importance to logic and the mysterious aspect of life as well. Otherwise, externally, everything will look methodical, but inwardly there will be an imbalance.

When we do something repeatedly, it naturally becomes a routine and a lack of awareness envelopes the performance of the action. It becomes mechanical. As a matter of fact, most people like to do things mechanically since it lifts the burden of thinking to some degree. Routine jobs such as brushing our teeth, showering, eating, most of our talking and so-called listening are mechanical. Perhaps the mechanical part of the mind is required to perform certain work. However, we should not allow that part of the mind to overpower us. As Amma puts it, "In the modern day world, the individual is not given the importance it should have. Only skills are valued. Human beings are pushed down to the status of mere machines." In contrast, the spontaneous part of the mind is pure and crystal clear energy. It is closer to the whole. Once we establish a connection with that part of the mind, it acts like a 'savior' in many difficult situations of life, not just in our personal and family life but in our professional life as well.

Beginning from the family and extending to one's work place, one of the most important traits a good leader should have is the capacity to see what is beneath the surface in all situations. In other words, we should develop a special talent and, with awareness, switch from the mechanical to the spontaneous part of the mind whenever appropriate. The difference in the operating system between the mechanical and the spontaneous is like forcibly opening a flower versus allowing nature to open it naturally. Amma says, "When we forcefully try to open a flower bud, its beauty and fragrance are lost. We destroy the flower. On the other hand, if we allow the flower to blossom naturally, its beauty and fragrance are fully revealed."

The unfolding of life happens only when we combine the logical and mysterious aspects in equal proportions. The problem is when we get stuck in our head, forgetting to fall back into our heart. Let's be adept in using both our head and heart. They are like our legs. Consider them equally and use them without leaning too much to one side. It will cripple us if we think, 'The right leg is more important than the left, or vice versa.' When you want to apply logic, do it fully, and when you want to be in the heart, be fully there. This is moment-to-moment living, or living in the present.

We live in a world where people are afraid to smile or even say a loving word to others because the mind equates everything with money. The thinking is that if I lend an ear to his problems, smile at him, or say a word to console him, he will end up asking for financial help.

There are people who help others when requested, but most people don't spontaneously reach out. A true leader is one who reaches out to the needy without hesitation and with no questioning of the logic of such a plan but with the loving heart of compassion.

This example shows how Amma uses her heart rather than logic. The year was 1989. We had been cherishing the thought of building the first prayer hall on the property. It was a long time dream about to come true.

The administrators of an orphanage in Kollam, Kerala had been struggling for years to provide for the children entrusted to their care, but they had reached the end of the line. All their funding had dried up, and they were faced with the imminent reality of having to turn the orphans and the other economically disadvantaged children out onto the street. As they were preparing to do so, someone suggested they try one last measure before resorting to the unthinkable. Some people told them to approach Amma and explain the predicament to her.

And so they came to Amma and described their dire situation. Hearing their plight, Amma immediately instructed that the funds that had been donated to construct her spiritual Center's first temple—the first proper building, in fact—be diverted to assume care of the orphanage. In doing so, she was laying the foundation for another kind of temple—a temple of compassion.

Amma could have easily thought that a temple was more important than taking over an orphanage with enormous liabilities accompanying it. Moreover, most people in India are greatly attached to temples. So, if they donate a sum to build a temple or prayer hall, they want to see that it is used for that purpose alone. If Amma had made a logical, calculative decision, she would have justified that the temple was long overdue and that the donated funds had been earmarked for that. Instead, she made a heartfelt decision that spontaneously moved the monies from the temple construction to the orphanage.

Today, that orphanage still stands, but it is unrecognizable compared to what was there before Amma assumed responsibility for the buildings, the grounds, and the children. When Amma's volunteers arrived, owing to the desperate financial condition of the previous administration, the children were in an extreme state of neglect and malnutrition, and the buildings were in a deplorable condition. There were even stories about the children doing wrong deeds such as stealing and being used by outside anti-social elements to fulfill their selfish motives.

In contrast, now the children are able to study and play in a safe, secure campus. This institution is now one of the more competitive schools because the children excel in music, sports and dance as well as academics. In state and local cultural competitions, they often win first prize. Amma's organization also ensures that the children build a strong culture of the heart while they are studying there. Additionally, more than 35% of them go on to pursue higher education with the cost fully sponsored by our NGO.

Booker T. Washington says, "Success in life is founded upon attention to the small things rather than to the large things; to the every day things nearest to us rather than to the things that are remote and uncommon."

There is a beautiful story about (Joseph) Rudyard Kipling, the famous British writer, poet, short-story writer, and novelist. He once bought a farmhouse on a hilly estate. He and his wife used to spend their vacations there, just to retreat from their busy city life. One morning, as the couple went out for a stroll, they met a very old woman, bent low with age, hobbling with the support of a stick. She was happily enjoying the fresh air and morning sun. When she saw Kipling and his wife, the old lady enquired, "Are you the people who bought the farmhouse on the hilltop?"

Kipling politely took off his hat and said, "Yes, ma'am."

"Are you staying there now?" the old lady again asked in a quavering voice.

This time, Mrs. Kipling replied, "Yes, Grandma."

"Then it must be your window that is so brightly lit up at night," said the woman.

"Oh yes!"

"Thank you! Oh thank you!" exclaimed the old lady. "You do not know—you cannot imagine—what a comfort those lighted windows are to me! You know I am old and lonely." She continued, "The lighted windows make me feel happy and cheerful."

"I'm so glad," said Mr. Kipling warmly, "You make us feel wanted and welcome in the neighborhood."

"I do hope you will stay there for a long time," said the woman anxiously. "And I do hope you will come here often."

"We do hope to, Ma'am," said Kipling.

"Oh good," said the woman happily. "Do keep those lights burning—they matter a lot to me!"

"We promise we will," said the distinguished writer.

A couple of days later when this caring couple left the farm after their brief vacation, they instructed the caretaker to remove the curtains of the windows and to keep the lights burning throughout the night, every night.

Amma says, "Little deeds of love, a kind word, a small compassionate act, all these create a change in you and others." So we should start with little deeds of love and kindness.

Chanakya, professor of economics and political science at the ancient Takshashila University and the author of the ancient Indian political treatise called *Arthasastra* (Economics) says, "The fragrance of flowers spreads only in the direction of the wind. But the goodness of a person spreads in all directions."

Chapter Eight

Flowing Like a River

When someone asks Amma whether the large number of people that always flock around her are her followers or disciples, Amma's response is, "Only mother and children are here, no guru, nor disciple." The relationship between mother and child is the only reciprocal love. It is like a circle. It keeps flowing and connecting.

This personal bond that Amma creates in peoples' hearts is one of the secrets of her success. As far as human relationships are concerned, the bond between the mother and child is the closest, the most powerful. The love, freedom, humility, and oneness we feel in the presence of our mother create the most spontaneous and natural relationship anyone can imagine.

Amma often compares herself to a river and its flow. She says, "I am like a river. Some people bathe in it. Some others wash their clothes in the river. There are people who worship the river. There are also people who spit in the river. But the river accepts everyone, discards none. It keeps flowing."

Suppose you express your appreciation for the services offered by a babysitter or housemaid. She will gratefully accept it. On the contrary, if it is your mother, provided she truly values the greatness of motherhood as a precious gift from God, she will say, "I haven't done enough for my child. There are still many things I can do for my baby." A mother's heart longs to do more and more for her child. Instead, if she boasts about the love and attention she has given to her child and makes claims of the sacrifice she has endured in the process of upbringing, her attitude is no more than that of a housemaid or a baby sitter who has expectations. In other words, all the care and concern has a price, whereas a mother has no expectations as she always thinks how much more she can do for her children.

Amma tells the story about a little girl who was admitted to the hospital. On the day she was to be discharged, the girl told her father, "The nurses had so much love and affection for me, even the attendants. At times it felt as though they loved me more than you and Mommy." At that point, the hospital staff handed the bill to the father. The little girl curiously asked, "What is that?" Her father responded, "It is the bill that shows the cost for all the love they have showered on you."

Om Saha Nau-Avatu|
Saha Nau Bhunaktu |
Saha Viiryam Karava-Avahai |
Tejasvi Nau-Adhii-Tam-Astu Maa Vidviss-Aavahai |
Om Shaanti Shaanti Shaantihi |

This is a popular peace mantra from the Upanishads. It means:
Om, May God Protect us Both (the Teacher and the Student),
May God Nourish us Both,
May we Work Together with Energy and Vigor,
May our Study be Enlightening, not giving rise to Hostility,
Om, Peace, Peace, Peace.

This mantra is normally chanted before starting a religious discourse or a scriptural class. The essence of the mantra, which is oneness and humility, has always been part and parcel of the *gurukula* system in ancient India. Though not prevalent today, the system still exists in some parts of the country in a much-modified form.

In ancient India, most of the gurukulas were situated in peaceful and secluded places where nature provided in abundance. Many of the teachers and masters of those days were house-holders who were endowed with heightened consciousness and maturity. Their wisdom and compassion were boundless. They were immensely experienced and knowledgeable about every single branch of science and philosophy. However, even though the masters were established in a state of perfection and content-ment, they had no ego. Therefore, the word, "Both" in the prayer is very significant. Even though the masters of yore had nothing to lose or gain, they remained humble and made the disciples feel completely relaxed, at home. The atmosphere that existed and the message they practiced was, 'There are no differences between us. I'm not superior to you. We are one, equals in the eyes of God.' This simple, yet profound lesson of 'humility and oneness' helped the students to develop a bond with the master. This enabled the students to remain completely open to the master and listen to his words with a receptive mind and heart. Thus, without a laptop, iPad/tablet, cellphone and even textbooks or notebooks, the teachers taught and the students learned, because it was a heart-to-heart communication, from the heart of the teacher into the heart of the student. The most powerful way of teaching was through example. With humility and love as guiding lights, with their head and heart hand-in-hand, both the teacher and the student worked together with a deep feeling of oneness.

"I have three precious things which I hold fast and prize. The first is gentleness; the second generosity; the third is humility,

which keeps me from putting myself before others. Be gentle and you can be bold; be generous and you can be liberal; avoid putting yourself before others and you can become a leader among men."

—Lao Tsu

Whether you are head of a family, chief of an organization, or leader of a country, if you have a caring attitude, humbleness in approach, and the inclination to sacrifice your own personal interests and comforts (thereby truly putting the needs of others ahead of yourself), you have the traits that make you matchless. Then you will be remembered, adored, and loved as someone who truly has no replacement. Your name and your actions will always remain as a guiding light to humanity.

According to ancient Indian tradition, the king was supposed to consider his subjects as his own family members and his country as his home. With all the mental and atmospheric pollution, this ancient concept is no longer practical. Though not in a literal sense, a CEO/leader, should consider employees as extended family as well. Giving a personal touch, a spirit of humaneness, is the real ingredient.

During the 2013 U.S. tour, when Amma was in Washington DC, Laurie Singh, a reporter, asked Amma, "You are in the U.S. Capitol today. Do you have a message for President Obama and his family?" Amma's answer wasn't a message for U.S. President Barack Obama alone but for all those who are in leadership positions all over the world, "The president belongs to the citizens of this country, belongs to the subjects, and his family is the entire country. May he serve this country as best as he can; may he have the deep understanding and the capacity to discharge his duties to take care of the people of this nation. May he and his family always be peaceful and happy."

Dave Packard, co-founder of Hewlett-Packard, originated the concept of '*Management by Walking Around* (MBWA),' which was featured in Tom Peter's book '*In Search of Excellence.*' Mr. Packard explained why he believed in the process of the manager walking around the office or plant and interacting with the employees. This technique not only helps the manager in getting a feel of the employee sector, but it also makes the employees feel cared for and connected to management.

In fact, while traveling within and outside India, Amma makes everyone joyful when she tours the various departments of her Centers. She visits the kitchen, construction sites, printing press, charitable hospitals, the cowshed, etc. At her headquarters in Kerala, Amma serves lunch each Tuesday for all the residents and guests. She eats with everyone, sings and dances with them, and answers their questions. Actually, this is an inseparable part of Amma's tour programs and daily activities. This atmosphere of intimacy and personal care is a source of tremendous support for her followers. It has a magical effect, enhancing people's level of enthusiasm and awareness. Additionally, during Amma's tours abroad, she serves dinner to all the people in attendance, and they are thrilled to receive their plate directly from Amma's hands.

There are times when Amma is at the headquarters or one of the branches, when she suddenly and unexpectedly walks around, checking each department, and making sure that the premises are kept clean and tidy. These inspections normally take place in the night, often past midnight. Regardless of the hour, as soon as Amma comes out of her room, residents surround her and join the tour.

During one of those 'Management by Walking Around (MBWA)' sessions, Amma suddenly stepped on a nail at a construction site. She picked up the nail and held it up in a way that everyone could see it clearly. In a serious voice Amma said, "See this. Don't you know that among the thousands of people who come here, there are many poor laborers depending solely on their daily wages to earn a livelihood? What if this nail causes an injury in the sole of one of those poor laborer's feet? In his ignorance about the seriousness of the wound, he may not even treat it. As the only 'bread-earning' member of the family, his staying back home to take rest means his wife and children will starve. So he will be forced to work regardless of the pain. This worsens the condition of the wound. It may even become septic, and the man will be bedridden for several weeks or even months. With no food and unable to fulfill even their basic requirements, his family will suffer. This is a potential scenario, right? Have you ever thought of this? Each one of us is responsible for the entire family's misery in case such a fate befalls one of the visitors. Due to our carelessness, our lack of concern for others, we turn out to be the cause or the source of the family's suffering. It is just a small nail, but it could make an unfortunate person's life miserable. Let me say this, if a similar incident happens again, I will take the responsibility of sweeping the premises and removing all the trash."

There are times when Amma sees sacks of leftover cement and pieces of bricks lying unattended. She immediately sits down and collects all of them and instructs the residents to use them for minor things like small slabs, pieces of cement blocks, or for filling and leveling purposes.

When Amma visits the kitchen and the vegetable chopping areas, first she goes straight to the huge trashcans. She does a close survey of their interiors and sometimes even sticks her hand into them. The purpose is to make sure that no food is wasted. If she finds the vegetable peels with too much edible food still on them, she immediately summons the veggie choppers. Showing what she found in the trash, Amma explains how, by wasting food, we deprive or even steal the food that rightfully belongs to a starving family. Then she demonstrates how to cut vegetables properly.

For some people, it is their habit to pick a leaf, pluck a flower, or nip a small branch from a plant or tree while walking by or standing and talking to someone. Every time Amma sees somebody doing this during her night rounds, she immediately reprimands the person saying, "You don't understand. They are sleeping. It's cruel to wake them up. Imagine what happens if someone shakes you vigorously while you are fast asleep. Wouldn't it give a jolt to you? Similar is the case with the plants and trees. Though inadvertently, you are also injuring a plant by picking its leaf for no reason." Amma then insists the person seek apology from the plant.

As a leader, Amma has perfect insight on how to exercise her authority without hurting others. She knows when and how to be a brilliant life coach, and she has perfect timing as to when to listen, when to put her foot down regarding a decision, and the precise time to give the silent treatment. But in the process of executing her managerial skills, Amma doesn't judge anyone or any situation. Hence, nothing affects her pleasant and cheerful mood. She uses emotions to express her feeling of being upset about something, and there are moments when she speaks in strong terms, but these are only masks, which she is capable of wearing or removing at any time. In essence, her nature is compassion and love. So, the purity of her intentions remains untouched. Management is not about walking around with an air of pride, showing off our ego, issuing orders and exercising our authority. It's about learning to be humble. Humility is the first step to good management.

Inspired by Amma's example, we have accomplished the target of zero waste at the headquarters of MAM. '*Reduce, Reuse and Recycle*' is Amma's motto.

In 2011, Amma launched a program called *Amala Bharatam, Clean India Campaign* (ABC). The goal was to create awareness in the general public about environmental cleanliness and the protection of nature. The program began with a big bang, and volunteers have been successfully implementing it since its inception. The cleanup event recounted below is a classic example of MBWA. Throughout the evening, Amma helped people see her as involved in the work and a part of the team.

During one segment of Amma's yearly North India tour, she visited Kolkata (Calcutta) in January 2013. It was a two-day program, January 19th and 20th. On both days Amma sat for over 12 hours continuously offering her iconic embrace to people. On the second day, in the middle of the session at about 6:00 pm, Amma announced that the road next to the Center where the program was being held had to be cleaned, and in this way the ABC would be launched in Calcutta. She sent volunteers to inspect the area that was to be cleaned and procure the necessary equipment for the cleaning operation.

When darshan finished at 11:00 pm, Amma got up from the stage and walked down the long driveway out to Budge Budge Trunk Road, the busy street that passes in front of the Center.

Along with 800+ volunteers, Amma then spent the next three hours cleaning 3 km of the road. Amma herself donned gloves and a mask and got right into the filth that had accumulated over the years along the roadside. The helpers fanned out along the roadside picking up garbage of all shapes, sizes, and smells, and they bagged it up for collection. After raking, shoveling and scraping up the trash from the pavement for three hours, Amma then walked the entire 3 km stretch of the road to observe all the volunteers hard at work and to show her appreciation for their efforts. On her way back to the Center, a large truck arrived to pick up all the bags of trash that had been collected.

Throughout the night, many local residents were roused from their slumber by the laughter and joy with which complete strangers from all over the world were cleaning the neighborhood. Many opened their doors and came out with stunned looks on their faces to see what this unexpected celebration was that was taking place outside in the cold night. The astonished police who came to escort Amma were helpful in directing the busy traffic on the road. The next morning when Amma and the tour group left for Odisha (the next stop on the tour), the road was completely spotless.

Since its launch, the Amala Bharatam project has held large clean up drives all over India. Several state governments across India have pledged their support for the Campaign and have sponsored clean up drives in their states.

The *Times of India*, one of India's leading English newspapers reported the news thus, "As part of the launch of ABC, Amma along with her hundreds of disciples and devotees swept and cleaned a three kilometer stretch of Budge Budge Road near

Sarkarpool. This was done in the late hours on January 19th after Amma gave darshan to thousands of devotees inside the Ashram."

As explained in the Sanskrit verse quoted at the beginning of the chapter, for Amma there is no 'I' and 'you.' The feeling 'I'm superior, you are inferior' is absent in her. Only 'us, we, mother and children' exist.

The Bhagavad Gita says, "Great people look with an equal eye on a scholar endowed with learning and humility, on a cow, on an elephant, and even on a dog and an outcast."

Amma says, "Learning is an endless process. So, always be a beginner, have a childlike attitude. Humility keeps your heart always full and lessens the ego."

Chapter Nine

Contentment, the Real Wealth

Amma says, "When you are only focused on action, not on the result, contentment simply arises. The moment your focus changes from action to the result, the joy and contentment leaves you in the hands of anxiety and fear. To be content means to be centered."

I'm not against money or riches, and my vision about life, which I learned from Amma, is also not in opposition to wealth. However, being wealthy and owning enormous riches involves an intrinsic problem. It is challenging to know whether you or your money is more sought after, whether the love is directed towards you or your money! The answer will remain ever elusive. Money is certainly a means, but you might want to contemplate whether or not to make it your end goal. The interesting thing is that if a happy person has a great deal of money, he will probably feel happier. Conversely, if he is wealthy but unhappy, he may become more sorrowful even while living in the midst of plenty.

The spiritual masters praised *tripti*—contentment. These wise men of olden times emphasized the importance of having contentment with regard to the possession of wealth. When they professed tripti as a virtue, they never meant it in terms of generation of wealth or accomplishments, simply the possession of it. "Go ahead and profit," they said, "but don't stake your contentment on it. Don't fall under the misconception that the generation of wealth and happiness are linked." However, an ignorant person who misunderstood the message decided this meant one shouldn't work, shouldn't strive hard to accomplish anything in life. This interpretation was never the intention of the spiritual masters.

Thus, we have created a false connection between money and happiness. If we have money, happiness follows; if not, happiness evades us. But in truth, this concept is wrong; it is created by our mind, the ego.

Contentment is in appreciating what we have, not craving for what we don't have. Once this false connection between money and happiness is severed, we realize that despite whether our annual income is US$30,000, US$100,000, or US$1,000,000, our happiness is not affected. In fact, it is from this attitude that the businessman gains the power to truly contribute to the nation's growth, because after establishing what he and his family needs, he can then use the rest to contribute to the nation—to the poor, to education, to housing, to disaster relief, etc.

So, we should figure out what we need and thereafter become philanthropic by looking beyond our own family to the world family. We should improve not only the home in which our children live but also the world in which they live.

Recently I met R.N. Ravi, a former IPS officer who had just retired from the post of Special Director to the Central Intelligence Bureau. Currently, he is the Advisor to the Ministry of Home Affairs. This very kind, well-respected gentleman and his wife adopted two children from the streets of Delhi and raised them along with their own three biological children. As he was sharing some of his experiences, he said to me, "I do things like this because it gives me so much joy, and it helps my heart to open up; I feel content. I believe in fate and karma, but I also believe in God's grace more than that. In my own life, God always shows me the right path, the things that I should be doing. He just uses us as his instruments."

Ravi narrated a beautiful incident that happened when he was serving as superintendent of police in one of the districts in Kerala. The officer, during his tenure in his district, instructed his subordinates to have complaint boxes placed throughout the various parts of the town. Ravi explained, "Anyone could post a letter, complain, or put a suggestion in the box, signed or unsigned. Every evening my staff used to collect them and bring them to me for further action. It helped us in extending better service to the people by reaching out to them rather than waiting for the people to come to the police, which is not always a pleasant experience for them. I thought my job was a divine commission to reduce and wipe tears from peoples' eyes as much as I could. The experiment drastically brought down the incidents of crime in the districts."

Once he received a note from a little boy that was placed in the box, "Police uncle, every day I wait by the side of the road for the school bus to come. In the hot sun the tar on the surface of road melts and it sticks to my shoes. Can police uncle do something about that?" Strictly speaking this is not at all part of his job of policing. He could have easily brushed the boy's request aside by giving some lame excuse. But the officer immediately called the local Public Works Department and requested them to repair that part of the road, which they did.

Ravi continued, "On another occasion, I received a letter from an elderly lady who lived in a local old age home. The content of the letter was, 'Son, several of us who are very old and sick live in an orphanage for old people. There is only one ceiling fan for all of us. It has been broken for several weeks now, and nobody cares about repairing or replacing it. Could you please help us?'"

Again it was not his area of responsibility. Like most people do, he could have thrown the letter into the trash and forgotten about it, but not this man. The officer bought a new fan. Taking an electrician along with him, the officer went to the old age home and fixed it for the residents. All of them, especially the one who wrote the letter, were extremely happy and thankful to him.

The officer told me, "I still keep these letters with me, keep those experiences in the treasure chest of my heart, and contemplate on them. It reminds me that just as I have a duty towards my own family, I also have a duty towards society, not only as a police officer, but as a human being, as someone sent by God to help others, in whatever capacity I have. I am *His* messenger, God's emissary. This realization gives me immense joy and contentment." In fact, each one of us is a messenger of God. This is an intelligent police officer, a professional, who applies more heart than head in his work.

"Every one entrusted with a mission is an angel." This was written by Maimonides, who was a Jewish philosopher, astronomer, one of the most prolific and influential Torah scholars, and a physician.

It is a mistake to think that the graph of our enjoyment will show a downward trend if we welcome the value of contentment to our lives. This is a misapprehension created by greed. Here, it's important to remember one thing. The ancient science of spirituality was never life negating; rather, it is life affirming. Throughout the history of mankind, there were tyrants (autocrats) who upheld this anti-contentment philosophy and even forced this idea upon their subjects, especially the intellectually weaker sections of society. However, the truth is, no genuine spiritual master, in the East or West, has ever had this approach towards life. They welcomed life with all its varied experiences. The difference is that they not only accepted happiness, success, and honor but also unhappiness, failure, and dishonor. They didn't curse others or nature while going through such experiences, but they fearlessly shouldered the responsibility of the situation, smilingly saying 'yes' to them. In short, they valued and welcomed both external and internal wealth equally. They appreciated the external wealth and the joy it provided, but with the same spirit, they also valued the internal wealth of contentment. This created a perfect balance in their lives. For them, enjoyment was most important.

One of the Indian scriptural texts, the *Taittiriya Upanishad*, gives a ten step graphical description of external wealth and contentment. Suppose a person moves from step 1 to step 2 in his process of gaining wealth. In a similar manner, another person raises his contentment level from step 1 to step 2. Now if you were able to measure the happiness level of both these people, you will find that the second person, by increasing his contentment level, is a hundred-fold more joyful than the first person engaged in amassing external wealth. Even without any modern gadgets, he will be much more content and much happier than a wealthy person who is not content.

Genuine contentment is the outcome of the unconditional help that we offer to deserving people. Helping others brings us happiness because when we serve someone without expecting anything back, we become more expansive. Our consciousness level increases. When we help someone selflessly, we identify with the other person's happiness or sorrow whether we are aware of it or not. In that process, we are actually seeing our self in the other person. The other becomes an extension of us, and the feeling of 'otherness' disappears.

There is a popular television show in the U.S. that offers an example of how helping others allows us to see our self in the other person. Some of America's most successful self-made millionaires are embarking on a truly incredible journey. They will spend a week in the country's poorest areas and ultimately reward some unsung community heroes with hundreds of thousands of dollars of their own money. Based on the hit UK television series of the same name, each episode of *Secret Millionaire* follows one of America's most successful business people for a week as they leave the comforts of home behind. They keep their true identities hidden while living in some of the country's most impoverished neighborhoods.

Residing in local housing on welfare-level wages, these "secret millionaires" try to find the most deserving people within the community. We're talking about those selfless individuals who continually sacrifice everything to help anyone in need and ultimately encourage others to do the same.

Amos Winbush III, without his usual clothes and a credit card, went to live in New Orleans at poverty level for a week on Secret Millionaire. Though he had built a multimillion-dollar company from the ground up, one of the hardest things Amos Winbush III had to do was live on US$30.50 a week for Secret Millionaire. "I went to a grocery store the first day and completely broke down," says the CEO of CyberSynchs, a New York City-based technology firm worth upwards of US$196 million.

"I bought bread, milk and cereal and realized that the bill was like 60 bucks. I had to put stuff back," says Winbush. "It was a huge eye-opener. This was my life for one week, but this is many peoples' life every day."

He says his experience changing lives in New Orleans has changed him. "I was kind of self-absorbed. When you have a start-up, you're really focused on growing your company, not necessarily looking at the person that's walking in front of you and wondering, 'How is their life?' That changed. I got back to the city completely renewed."

Throughout this incredible experience, the millionaires come face-to-face with some truly extraordinary people who put their own needs aside for the sake of others. At the end of the journey, they reveal their true identity and donate their own money to these local heroes. It's a life-changing moment.

Recently I met a small group of ladies who shared an inspiring ongoing story with me. They are basically from lower middle class families. They are part of *Amritakudumbam*, a wing of Amma's spiritual activities. Just as the name signifies, each Amritaku-dumbam is made up of several families who come together to do spiritual practices and service to society. Coming from poor families, these ladies toil the whole day to make ends meet. The story they shared with me brought tears to my eyes. Every day they save a meager amount from their daily wages, and once in two weeks, they buy rice and vegetables with the money thus saved. They cook the food and take it to the nearby orphanage to feed the poor children there. I would say that their consciousness and contentment level is much higher than the wealthiest person in the world. These ladies were following Amma's teaching, "Offer what we can to society." Their love for God raised their consciousness level, which, in turn, changes the outside circumstances.

When we stake our happiness on wealth, on domination, on becoming the next Bill Gates, then not only will we have stress, we will become stress itself. We will never know peace. No matter how rich we become, our life will be hell. It will be full of fear. If we stake our happiness on the stock market, our happiness and peace will be at the market's mercy. And we all know how the market is—up and down, up and down, up and down. Imagine the mental state of someone who has risked his happiness on such a market? He will be like an insane person. The market's up, and he is dancing with joy. The market crashes, and he is jumping out the window. Why? He wagered his happiness on something that, by its very definition, fluctuates mercilessly.

As we all know, the world, by definition, is unstable and unpredictable—be it the world of family, the world of business, or even the world of love. Contentment comes from our inner power—the power to think and feel positively. And this is where spirituality comes into our lives. It keeps us centered and balanced, which then in turn, allows us to play—without fear—in the unstable and unpredictable world.

> *"There is no austerity equal to a balanced mind, and there is no happiness equal to contentment; there is no disease like covetousness, and no virtue like mercy."*
>
> —Chanakya

Chapter Ten

The Hidden Strength of Sorrow

When a company doesn't encourage a culture of the heart among its employees, the result could be a divisive outbreak of conflict. Workplace conflict is quite common in almost all organizations. Because companies have an assortment of people from various cultures, backgrounds, nationalities, and languages, disputes and differences of opinion are inevitable. Differences in educational qualifications, intellect, religious preference, and deep-seated emotions also contribute to the intensity of these conflicts.

In a speech Amma gave at the UNAOC meeting in Shanghai, she said, "Irrespective of which country, harmony and unity can exist in society only when culture and modernization go hand and hand. Otherwise, mutual trust will be destroyed. The failure to harmonize culture and modernization will give rise to many different communities and groups that will eventually assert their rights divisively. This will only create groups filled with hatred for each other, remaining completely disconnected like isolated islands. In order for a society of diverse traditions to remain peaceful and successful, its people should try to grow and evolve, while simultaneously acknowledging the traditions that have been passed down through the generations. History has taught us that innovation in disregard of tradition will only result in immediate satisfaction and short-lived prosperity."

How does one resolve these kinds of conflicts? 'Let the warring parties resolve it themselves' is the first step, but when things are on the verge of getting out of control, the leader has to step in. If not addressed in an intelligent, caring, polite, and diplomatic manner, such situations can spread to other areas of the organization affecting the work place environment and the team's productivity. It could also undermine the morale of the workers.

Some experienced employees may leave if the resolution of a dispute is delayed. No one wants to work in an extremely stressful or an unfriendly environment. Being a well coordinated, meticulous, and systematic worker is one thing, but mentally preparing yourself to face challenging situations every day is an entirely different thing. For an untrained and ill-equipped mind, workplace survival can be an energy dissipating exercise.

I have been travelling all over the world with Amma for most of the last 34 years. Part of my *seva* (duty) is to sit next to Amma's chair and translate people's questions as they come to Amma in the question line or occasionally when they are in line to receive their hug. I have seen how people spontaneously open up and pour out their hearts to Amma while she embraces them. Amma patiently listens to their personal, professional, physical, emotional, and spiritual problems and recommends solutions. It is really shocking and sometimes even depressing to know the amount of grief and extreme sadness that people carry within. But I also see how people transform, how their acceptance level grows, and their happiness takes on a new dimension after sharing their problems with Amma.

One of the major issues people discuss with Amma is about the tussle, inner and outer, they go through at their workplaces and the immense mental strain, emotional stress, and physical exhaustion it causes. A majority of them say, 'By the time I get back home in the evening, there is no energy or enthusiasm left.' 'Straight to bed' is the routine many of them follow.

The workplace problems begin with the early morning commute from home to work after taking care of the family's necessities and continues throughout the day with such frustrations as workplace politics, bias shown to the 'boss's pet,' an incompetent manager, etc. The list is long. If this state of affairs is left unattended, the inner conflict rapidly becomes evident in outside interactions. This conflict affects the output of the workers and soon reflects on the entire company in the form of union strikes, boycotts, shutdowns, and so forth. The solution lies in the manager's understanding and his or her capability of nipping problems in the bud.

There are things that we cannot see with our external eyes. A leader, as he matures and becomes seasoned, should work to develop an intuitive eye. This means a clarified or refined inner eye through which one is capable of seeing things inside out. That eye will catch subtle things missed by the external eyes. A weathered manager helps the employees see their limitations and weaknesses, thereby creating necessary awareness. Real support is not only in offering attractive wage and benefit packages, but also in having a deep understanding of the talents, skills, and fragilities of the team members.

Helping employees process emotions is a sensitive task that must be accomplished in a healthy manner. Emotions should be treated with utmost care, like unfolding a flower, as mishandling this important aspect could have a negative impact on all areas of life including family relationships and health. Of course, managers and employees do have outside experts such as competent psychologists, therapists, and counselors to guide them through these situations and give them a wider perspective.

Some suggestions counselors give are:

- Be patient and focus on your work.
- Do some introspection and self-analysis.
- If your boss hires an unqualified manager or a close peer of his who does not have the necessary skills and talents, try to see things from the new manager's perspective. Through gentle reminders and corrections, try to bring his shortcomings to his attention.
- Don't compare. Recognize and understand the skills and weaknesses of others and accept them as they are.
- Don't judge.
- Encourage congruency of goals and team up for the success of the organization.
- Try to work on your own weaknesses first.

All of these suggestions work, but only to a certain extent. There are always pros and cons. Ultimately, it is a change in the employee's perception that really works. They can change companies and jobs. Or else, as some people do, they can also start their own business where they are their own boss. However, whatever solutions they consider, these shadows will follow them everywhere because wherever they go, they are going to view and evaluate situations with the same mind.

Amma says, "In life there are two types of situations: where we have the choice to fix the problem and where we are left with no choices. When there is a choice, we can work harder and harder until we accomplish the goal. On the contrary, in certain other situations, no matter how much we struggle, it is not going to help us, and we will end up completely defeated. Suppose we are only 5 feet tall and we would like to be half an inch taller. We may take multi-vitamins, or hang upside down by our ankles, or do other stretching exercises. In this case, all our efforts will be futile. It is only a waste of our precious time and energy because the DNA constituting our body has already decided our height. So here we have to accept the situation and move on. But if we fail in an exam or in an interview, we do have a choice to retake the exam or appear for another interview until we succeed. The difference between these two examples should be well understood. Otherwise, it will cause agonizing pain and fear."

We should leave no stone unturned until we come to a point when the gentle voice of our conscience instructs us, 'You have done everything you can. Now stop and relax.' Trust that voice. In fact, trust only that voice. What is the point in fighting a situation where you will eventually end up losing the fight and feeling humiliated and totally exhausted? Allow this understanding to go deep within. For this to happen, a mere self-examination is not enough. It requires deep meditation. Only meditation can create the necessary space and silence within to replenish the lost energy and prevent further energy loss. Real acceptance, which is the positive outlook and the inner strength we are searching for, may not come as quickly as we want. Just as constant effort is fundamental to any accomplishment, sincere and continuous effort is required to attain this attitude of acceptance. That said, I should also say that going through the experience is sometimes needed to reach that point of relaxation and revelation. But as we go through the experience, we should remain as open as we can and not allow the experience to overwhelm or overpower us. It's not easy, but it is certainly possible because we have the inner potential, and actually, we have infinite capacity.

Let me share an experience: In 1999, I suddenly developed a severely prolapsed cervical disc followed by an intense period of pain and suffering as well as emotional turmoil. Amma was the first to warn me, even before the initial symptoms manifested. We were on the annual North India tour. As always, the entire tour was by road. Just after a hugely crowded evening program in Bangalore which lasted until late the next morning, Amma got into the car to leave for the next venue. I was in the front seat next to the driver. Soon after the car moved and picked up speed, I felt Amma's gentle touch on my shoulder. The vibration of the touch was different than normal. I looked back. Amma smiled, but there was sadness in her smile. In a soft voice she said, "I feel as if something ominous is hovering around you." Her whisperings, the eyes, her touch, and the whole vibration were powerful enough to convey an unknown message that was yet to unfold.

The very next day I developed a pain in my shoulder blade. It started small, like a sprain, and then gradually grew worse day by day. In a couple of days, the pain moved down my right arm. By the time we reached Pune, the pain was intolerable. I couldn't lift my arm, sit, stand, or even lie down. Finally Amma instructed me to have an MRI. The MRI showed a prolapsed cervical disc with the disc compressing a nerve. The doctors we consulted unanimously recommended surgery. Amma did not agree. She said, "No surgery is required. Just take rest; it will heal by itself." This happened fourteen years ago. In those days, there was some trepidation about the recommended surgery in India. Anyhow, I decided to listen to Amma's instructions and rest.

For two months I couldn't move out of bed. It was not just the physical pain but the agonizing mental and emotional pain as well. When another specialist shared some scary sounding information about the potential after effects of the prolapsed disc, my emotional and mental condition was aggravated further. My main concern was that I wouldn't be able to continue the *seva* which I had been doing for the last twenty years. For two decades, I had remained fully and vigorously active.

I thought I had no fear. There was no trace of fear in my conscious mind. However, this experience was a major event in my life, as everything seemed to be falling apart as though it was the end of my life. There was pitch darkness with no light "at the end of the tunnel." Everything was going smoothly, and then this thing hit me like a thunderbolt. The passing of each moment was like a journey through ages. Helpless as I was, all that I could do was cry profusely; I shed buckets of tears every day and prayed with all my heart for inner strength, love, and faith.

Like a celebrated psychologist *par excellence*, Amma guided me through every step of the experience, instilled faith and confidence, and helped me to overcome the fear. Even so, it took over six months to move out of the darkness that had enveloped me.

However, I had to take the first step and keep moving forward. Whether it is an outside situation or an emotional upsurge, the first step we take is most important. Self-love is the first step. Don't mistake self-love as love for our ego. Rather it is faith in our own self, our inner potential. To further elaborate on this, it is the firm faith in the gift of life. Our birth is not accidental; it has a purpose, a higher goal. We are here to accomplish something no one else can do. Without us, there will be a gap in the universe. The universe will miss us. Be convinced of this.

The second step, which is equally important, is to find the right guide, a mentor who has a comprehensive vision of life, has experienced every bit of it, and is a true benefactor of society.

Once you achieve these two steps, the third step, celebrating the joy of life without becoming obsessed with external conditions, will automatically spring forth.

I found Amma as my leader and guide. She sheds light on my path. I just have to have the willingness to walk the path. She helped me manage my emotions and learn from the pain so that my body could heal.

Each one of us needs a leader who can lead us by example, not just a scholarly, knowledgeable person with tons of accumulated information. With the big leaps in the field of science and technology, anyone can be a scholar in today's world. It is just a mouse click away. What I mean to say is that we must look for a mentor gifted with true wisdom who is capable of teaching and training by example and spontaneity. An Albert Einstein quote will shed light onto this, "Setting an example is not the main means of influencing others; it is the only means."

Aid from a leader with the aforesaid qualities will give us the courage, discernment, precision, vision, and right perspective. This change in the inner world creates a change in the outer situations as well.

We may win a lottery and become a multi-millionaire. Or, as one of the four final contestants of a reality show, we may win the first prize and get a million dollars as prize money. But that is not going to bring about any real change in us. Of course, we will buy a better house, a better car, a bigger plasma TV, as much gold as we want, and so forth. But as a human being, we will continue to act rooted in the same mental patterns, conditioned by our mind and its negativities.

Instead of killing ten or twenty-five people with a wooden club or hammer, one person can now kill thousands by pressing a button. And we call it scientific development! Is that real change? My point is: What needs to be changed is our presence, the quality of our inner being, our total personality as a human being. Whatever change happens in our life, it should help diminish our problems. The change should be qualitative, not quantitative. It can be quantitative also, if we wish so. But, it should not aggravate the existing problems.

One point to always keep in mind is that every occurrence, no matter whether it is inner or outer, has a center, a heart. There you will find a precious message. We have two choices. We can either sensationalize it or be sensitive to it. It is not a vulnerable sensitivity I am talking about, but rather a penetrating sensitivity. What does penetrating sensitivity mean? It is the power to see through the pain and reveal the center of it. As *Kathopanishad*, one of the major *Upanishads* says, "One who is able to look within will experience the inner self, the center." Even though the verse talks about rediscovering the center of our true existence, it is applicable to all experiences of life.

Looking within will uplift the whole experience to an entirely different dimension. We can see the subtlest aspects of the issue that remain hidden to others. Just by beholding and imbibing those principles, we are enabled to witness the environment, and our actions gain an extraordinary beauty, power, and charm.

It is a fundamental principle of life that individuals, alone, have to face all the experiences that life brings to them. However, if we have a leader, a living example of virtues and values as our guide, she will help us navigate through the seemingly treacherous waves of life. I am reminded of Ralph Waldo Emerson's words, "If you would lift me up, you must be on higher ground."

The pain-ridden periods of our life, the trying times, have greater depth than the moments we allege as happy because our happiness is momentary. These moments are skin deep. When people are seeking immediate satisfaction, what more can be expected?

We often think sorrow is a weakening emotion. However, those who have realized the mysteries of life set their own life as an example to convey the message that sorrow has a hidden strength. In fact, sorrow has a depth which happiness lacks. It's like night and day. Darkness has an impenetrability. If we develop the inner strength to penetrate the dense layer of our sad and sorrowful experiences, it will open up a new world of consciousness, and we will be handed the access key to a meaningful world of knowledge.

Amma's life is a perfect example to demonstrate the transformative power of sorrow, the metamorphosis that one can attain. Once we understand this secret, then each time we come face to face with sorrow, that darkness aspect disappears and light alone remains. It will be a simultaneous experience; hence, we should not disregard pain. Instead, we must accept pain, and that acceptance brings light. This insight gives a greater dimension to life. The whole meaning that we have given to life (earn more and spend more) will undergo a change. Our body, mind, emotions, and even the wealth that we earn become powerful tools to create the change we envision.

The profound message we learn when we have such a leader is that life's pains are not to weaken us but to awaken us. Sorrows are not to make us feel sad or depressed but to help us become more aware. Failures are not to stop us but to unleash our inner power.

Amma gives an example, "Suppose we are walking in the dim light of dusk, and a thorn punctures the sole of our foot. We remove the thorn and proceed, but now we are more cautious, looking for additional thorns. Suddenly we see a cobra, a poisonous snake. Our awareness due to the thorn helped to avert a potentially dangerous situation. Had we not been alert, the cobra might have bitten us. The thorn piercing our foot should not be seen as a pain-ridden experience in this context. You may curse the thorn, but later when you look back and take a deeper look into that experience, you will realize that it helped to bring you to awareness."

Two quotes of Charlie Chaplin are worth mentioning here. He says, "Nothing is permanent in this wicked world, not even our troubles." And the other one is, "To truly laugh, you must be able to take your pain and play with it!" But it probably took Charlie Chaplin an entire lifetime to get a glimpse of this truth. The question that we need to ask ourselves is, 'Do I have to wait that long for this truth to dawn on me?'

Chapter Eleven

Multiple Lessons

"I like to think that a lot of managers and executives trying to solve problems miss the forest for the trees by forgetting to look at their people – not at how much more they can get from their people or how they can more effectively manage their people. I think they need to look a little more closely at what it's like for their people to work there every day." I don't know exactly what Mr. Gordon Bethune, the retired U.S. airline executive and former CEO of Continental Airlines, meant when he made this insightful comment. Nevertheless, it appears this man understood some of the aspects of keeping his team members in good spirits.

Peter Drucker hit the right note when he said: "Most of what we call management consists of making it difficult for people to get their work done."

Consciously or unconsciously, some of today's managers and leaders assume an uncalled-for seriousness and an air of pride as if the whole world should know that they hold a powerful position. Puffing up our ego and attempting to be weighty will not add anything positive to our personality, nor will it make us a good leader or manager. Conversely, it may even negatively affect our reputation and productivity.

It is said that in management and leadership, it is advantageous to be friendly with people, but disadvantageous to make friends with them. In this regard, Amma says, "A responsive non-attachment is what we should practice. Be open, but aloof. Be one among them, but be alone." It sounds like a puzzle. Nonetheless, this is one of the secrets of success; be close to people but be distant as well.

When we are getting too close to people, situations can blindside us, make us unconscious of the truth. This closeness or familiarity will negatively influence our sense of judgment. Above all, we may become completely exposed. In a moment of excitement, sometimes we slip into a mood of forgetfulness. In the flash of that moment, we lose track of our own identity. We tumble into a state of unawareness. In that instant of identification with a particular situation, we may utter a word, display a gesture, make a sign, or show a facial expression that we may consider insignificant. But, for a really high-pitched person, the simple sign could serve as a clear indicator. If he has been waiting for the right opportunity to derail our career, he will use it to go up the ladder, pushing us all the way down. It can tear down an entire empire built upon our sweat and blood, all because of a single moment when we were not mindful.

The superficial mind is incapable of achieving anything. All accomplishments are babies born out of the deeper mind, a special womb created within to conceive of innovative ideas. Knowledge is not external. It is not out there. It is internal, a part of our being. The popular saying, '*The eyes are the windows to the soul*,' can be slightly modified to, 'Our eyes become a new window to behold an entire world of knowledge within, the unleashed potential dormant in us.'

Normally, people confuse the meaning of these two words: aloneness and loneliness. Many even think they are the same. While aloneness elevates us to a higher state of consciousness, mindfulness, expansiveness and cheerfulness, loneliness pushes us down to unawareness, a contracted state of mind, and unhappiness. How can an unhappy manager be creative or productive? Will his employees appreciate his grumbling nature? Will such a person be able to establish interdepartmental communication? Will a manager who belongs in this category be able to lovingly receive and give much-needed, honest feedback?

When we become accustomed to something, often it is similar to taking on those same characteristics, becoming more like that person or thing. "Fight back in the same coin" is the accepted rule in our world today. The message is, 'If the world is unfair, we, too, should follow suit.'

"*The Difficulty of Being Good,*" the title Gurucharan Das, Indian author and intellectual, had chosen for his book, sounds appropriately named. Agreeing to be good and honest in all circumstances is, indeed, difficult. Nonetheless, aren't all accomplishments difficult? Moreover, 'good' is not superlative. It doesn't mean perfect. To be the finest is, of course, a challenging goal. But with all our emotional imperfections and weaknesses, it is still possible to be a good human being if we really want to be. While minds all over the world think the same negative thoughts, to minimize and reduce the intensity of those thoughts is achievable. We can also refrain from acting on undesirable and destructive thoughts, though it is almost impossible to block them out completely.

People become accustomed to having problems. However, some times such people, while going through their own problems, give the problem to others as well. I recall one of Amma's examples: "A man had a severe migraine headache, and he complained about it endlessly to everyone in his family, even to his friends and neighbors. By the end of the day, the man's headache was gone, but everyone else had a headache."

It is normal for us to be too attached to our wealth and possessions. If there is the minutest sign or doubt that someone might steal or snatch them away, it can create turbulence in our mind. In a similar manner, people can also become attached to their problems and ideas.

> *I read the following Rules of a Toddler:*
> *If I like it, it's mine.*
> *If it's in my hand, it's mine.*
> *If I can take it from you, it's mine.*
> *If I had it a little while ago, it's mine.*
> *If it's mine, it must never appear to be yours in any way.*
> *If I'm doing or building something, all the pieces are mine.*
> *If it looks just like mine, it's mine.*
> *If I think it's mine, it's mine.*

All our creations are a product of our limited mind. Hence they are not going to be utterly flawless. But if we are overly attached to our plan, our 'baby,' we are following the above 'Rules of a Toddler.' In that state of mind when we are too attached, we will not be able to hear the feedback and suggestions made by our team; we cannot do justice to our team.

I have heard people say, "Life is unfair, but I am getting used to it."

Amma's view is different. She tells people, "Life seems to be unfair only when perceived with our external eyes. Observe it from within and we realize that life is always fair, because life is the totality, the cosmos. People can be unfair, but the cosmos ought to be fair, since it is equally available to everyone, but we should always remain well-rooted in our own deep convictions about the values of life."

Amma's approach is to not get used to the ways of the 'unfair' world, thus not following in the footsteps of unfairness. Unavoidable and inevitable are the world's ways. Go through the experiences with courage, but learn to transcend them. Transcending is transforming—transforming our weaknesses and limitations into strengths. Thus we rise above and remain untouched by the unfair world.

Because 'Love all, Serve all. Give, Forgive, and be Compassionate' are the underlying principles of Amma's management style, there are no difficulties in giving feedback to any member of her team at anytime. The most powerful and attractive part of such a feedback session is that just as anyone else on the team, Amma also takes equal responsibility for the situation. If someone says, "It is all my fault," Amma's response would be, "No, your mistake is my mistake. Perhaps, I did not pay proper attention to the details."

Rather than using such occasions to take the person or group involved to task, Amma always tells them to be more conscious and more aware in the future. She motivates them by helping them to perceive the whole incident from another point of view.

Let me share an incident to illustrate this point. This experience occurred much before credit cards were introduced. Our purchasing team always had to carry cash on them in order to do the shopping for the NGO headquarters. The team consisted of three young men including the driver who was also a resident/ volunteer. In one such shopping trip, all the cash, quite a huge amount, somehow was lost. They were either pickpocketed, or the money was misplaced. When the youngsters returned, they were not brave enough to face Amma. The team was afraid Amma would be angry, so they sheepishly remained behind the closed doors of their rooms. Very soon, another volunteer was sent to fetch them. Amma wanted to see them was the message. Of course, they were gripped by fear and guilt, but Amma welcomed them with a big smile on her face. She asked them to sit next to her. Caressing them, Amma said, "Take it easy. Don't worry. It happens. It is not your fault. So, relax. I'm not upset at all. Hopefully the money went to a deserving person."

The words were simple. The attitude was thoughtful. Together Amma's caring words had a profound impact on the team. For them, it was like entering an air-conditioned room after being in the scorching heat of the sun for a long time. They were obviously touched and put at ease.

When things settled, Amma told them, "Slip-ups are normal. I have absolutely no difficulty forgiving and forgetting. But even a penny is extremely valuable for me. It is like a drop, but drops constitute the river. Every penny, combined with our efforts, must be returned to society as our offering, as a much bigger package. There are three types of mistakes: happening, doing, and purposeful. Sometimes things go wrong even when we are attentive and careful. This is a happening. We did not do it consciously with intention. But when something goes wrong due to our carelessness, it is an unconscious doing. The third category involves mistakes that are committed purposefully or with intention. These mistakes are committed consciously. All three will be given chances to improve, but not indefinitely. Whether or not a mistake is committed knowingly or unknowingly, it does have a common factor—lack of awareness. There is no point in even committing mistakes if they are not corrected using the opportunities provided. Remember that." The feedback was very well received.

The whole thing was communicated in a gentle yet penetrating way, but only after the team was helped to overcome their tense mental condition. That was the first step. Once relaxed and open, the team's attention was directed towards the second step. Had the order been reversed, not even a word of the instructions would have been received as the team was wrapped inside the cocoon of fear and guilt.

Amma says, "The past is fact. Learning from it and having faith in the present will enable us to befriend the future." In fact, the future is the blossoming of the present. The entire contribution of the future depends on how intelligently we handle the present. So, let's move out of the irreversible facts and prepare to face the future by being in the present.

By not playing the normal blame game we see in the world, Amma resolves a situation without creating any guilt and feeling of unworthiness in others. Her 'warriors' are fully aware of this approach, and therefore, they totally open up to her. Thus, no detail, even the minutest, is ever missed.

It is observed by management experts that in many organizations one of the major gridlocks is giving and receiving feedback. Either it is inadequate or it is much delayed. In fact, rarely is feedback given in proper intervals. Fear of criticism, lack of confidence, obsession with one's own ideas, reluctance to face a competitor, or deep-seated hatred towards an immediate boss can be a few of the many impediments to giving and receiving valuable feedback at the right time and with the right attitude.

Authentic feedback is not a faultfinding journey. It respects and supports others' views. The remarks are also shared with complete honesty. It is more of an exchange, an interaction, a communication between two mature people or parties. The intention is to take the right decision that will benefit the organization. Unless both the giver and receiver mentally position themselves as people who evaluate and offer strategies from their perception, not as absolute solution finders, it is difficult to get healthy and productive feedback.

Dale Carnegie, an American writer and lecturer and the developer of many famous courses in self-improvement, salesmanship, and corporate training observed, "Any fool can criticize, condemn and complain ... and most fools do."

Amma has a unique manner of giving and receiving feedback. It is part and parcel of everything that happens around her and is not just limited to the institutions and humanitarian programs. Every single day, Amma either talks to the heads of departments directly or via the phone. She gets regular updates. As a recipient, Amma remains completely open and listens to everything that the giver has to say. And when it comes to sharing her views, Amma deeply analyzes every single piece of information, takes every comment into consideration, weighs the pros and cons right in front of her team, making sure that no vital factor is left out before reaching a conclusion. However, she unmistakably knows what to highlight and what not to—the aspects that can be openly discussed and the ones that are confidential.

Amma says, "Remember, two things are most important, truthfulness and the inner strength to hold secrets. Be truthful and never disclose a secret to another." This is one piece of advice that almost every member of her team receives.

Even though Amma runs the whole show of skillfully managing the institutions and humanitarian activities of our NGO, she is also totally unpretentious about it. She has absolutely no problem in personally talking to the various heads of departments, and she listens, interacts, and receives feedback from the most junior staff members as well. Even people who are engaged in menial jobs can freely approach Amma and lay out their problems and views to her.

I have witnessed several occasions when Amma discusses certain things with school children and gets their feedback. Once I asked her, "Why do you talk to these little kids about serious matters such as this?" Amma smiled and said, "Children are smarter than grownups. They may come up with brilliant ideas and lively examples. Never underestimate anyone. The universe's knowledge is bursting forth from all around. The search should be endless. Knock on every door. You never know the hidden sources. Outwardly it may look most simple and inconsequential. But remove the cover, and we may find a whole treasure inside."

Adhering to a specific working pattern and being strict about everyone following the rules unfailingly cripples a manager and the overall functioning of a company or department. Discipline is essential, but an amalgamation of work combined with fun will ensure open communication. In Amma's words, "Life should be a perfect combination of discipline and playfulness. Be serious and playful. Be both like an office and a forest. Discipline comes from the intellect and playfulness from innocence. When these two factors blend, it brings love and success."

Picture a systematic office merged with the beauty and whole-some feeling of a refreshing forest—it would uplift everyone's spirits. Create the opportunity. It is surprising to see how even the acutely snobbish and reserved among the team members suddenly open up. The conventional atmosphere in an office doesn't encourage people to talk naturally or to get to know each other. By creating special occasions for the team to get away from the office pressures and express their natural talents, a releasing and recharging effect is created. If these sessions are organized in the proper manner, it will bring out the hidden playfulness, the child within us in all its fullness and vigor. By forgetting our social, official, and family status as well as subordinate and superior feelings, we become equals, at least for some time. This, in turn, enhances the team's morale, creativity, productivity, and communication skills. A feeling of oneness is cultivated.

Amma is an expert in generating such a blend. The Chancellor, Amma, Vice-Chancellor, Medical Director, Deans, Head of Research Teams, Engineers, Administrators, Janitors, Canteen in-charges, Servers, Cleaners, Sweepers, Sound System Operators, Professionals from other areas, Westerners, and Indians all sit together. People are not categorized. She doesn't say, "I will only interact with the Deans or the Medical Director." She values the humanness in everyone and mingles with every one of her people. Each one of the team members gets the feeling, 'I am her most favorite. She really cares for me.' Any possible mental block is thus removed, and the person happily applies his full potential in his respective area of action, thereby opening all windows to give and receive feedback.

Those who have known life and its mysteries agree upon one point—that one should be full of heart regardless of what is being accomplished. It is really a question of our attitude towards what we do. And with a change of attitude, with work turning into a celebration, the whole setting of life changes.

When Amma travels in India and abroad, hundreds of people travel with her in several buses and other vehicles. We carry our own kitchen tent, the required utensils, big cooking vessels, plates, cups, chairs, sound system, etc. When the entourage reaches the program venue in each city, the volunteer staff members set up everything and start cooking very early in the morning. It's an all day through late night affair. One who visits these kitchens at Amma's program venues in India and abroad will have a tangible experience of how work can be transformed into real worship. These kitchens are places of festivity.

The Europe and Northern India tours are in the beginning of winter. In almost all cities, the kitchen is in tents outside the main hall. But, the atmosphere is ecstatic; people sing and dance. To them it feels as though they are not really working yet they are working very hard, but there is no tension. Rather, the playfulness imbued into the work acts as an antidote for any tension or negativity. If you ask for a logical explanation for such a joyful experience, to be frank, there is none.

Every year Amma's North America tour begins on the 3rd week of May. Before leaving, Amma does something special for the nearly 3000 residents of the Center in India. Together with the cooks and residents, she makes *masala dosas* (pancakes made from a mixture of powdered rice and black gram, stuffed with a thick paste of potatoes and big onions and spices) and french fries for everyone there. It sounds simple, but a close observation reveals a profound lesson in multitasking. The whole event happens under Amma's strict supervision. All the utensils are arranged well in advance in the main prayer hall. There will be huge gas stoves, a number of giant-sized dosa pans, spatulas, and bronze vessels to make french fries with boiling hot oil in them.

Right after the evening prayers, Amma commences the dosa and french fries party. Along with the cooks and residents, Amma actively participates in the cooking process and at the same time, she oversees every aspect of the task such as the quantity of oil added and maintaining as much uniformity as is possible in the sizes of each dosa and the potato slices. There will be constant reminders to be watchful so that the dosas and french fries are not over cooked. The prayer hall will be packed with little children, boys and girls, women and men of all ages and from all parts of the world. Some people will be making dosas, others french fries.

The entire crowd is eager to participate in the event. The excitement sometimes causes a slight disciplinary problem, particularly with the little children. Amma will ask them not to come too close to the boiling hot pans in a loving and affection-ate manner. If they don't listen, she raises her voice slightly. You will see Amma trying to calm the children down, and the next moment her attention turns towards the cooks in order to give instructions. And all this happens while she is also engaged in actually making dosas or cutting potatoes.

The month of May is still the peak of summer in Kerala and the prayer hall is not air-conditioned. Therefore, in addition to the accumulated heat of the scorching daytime sun, the temperature in the hall soars due to the heat, smoke, and fire emanating from the gas stoves, boiling oil, and hot dosa pans. The big gathering makes it worse. In short, the temple hall becomes a virtual furnace. But, there is so much exhilaration and festivity in the atmosphere that no one really bothers about the heat.

As the cooking progresses, Amma will begin to serve. Each person will get a couple of masala dosas and sufficient french fries. Amma personally hands them out to each resident, including little children. Even while serving the food, Amma meticulously watches every single detail of that action. In the midst of serving, if the quantity of the french fries is a little less on one plate, if a dosa is a little smaller than the one before, Amma will notice it and send the plate back asking for more. Thus, both quality and quantity controls are closely scrutinized and taken care of. Children, boys and girls, elderly people, those with digestion problems and other illnesses will have separate plates, depending on their age and appetite. So, zero waste is assured.

This anti-wastefulness policy is normal in all areas of Amma's institutions. 'No waste' is one of Amma's cherished mottos. Just as every administrative or management area matters, this area, too, has her constant personal attention. Amma says, "Always remember the millions of people who are thrown in the midst of poverty and starvation. Think of their suffering, their sad faces. When you waste even a morsel of food, you are depriving them of what they actually deserve. And when you take more than what you need, you are in fact stealing what is rightfully theirs."

As we reach the end of the 'dosa-fries party,' Amma leads everyone in a few songs. In a normal situation, thousands of people sitting jam-packed in a place with almost everyone bathed in sweat from the heat would be considered a physical suffering. However, here, every single individual—people of all ages, gender, cultures, religious faiths, nationality and language—thoroughly enjoys the experience. It is truly a festive atmosphere. Nobody is bothered about the inconveniences.

Cooking for thousands of people, maintaining quality and quantity, and serving with everything happening in the same place is not an easy task to manage. But here you see how work becomes worship, an event of celebration. People are brimming with joy. It is like watching the most enchanting dance.

The whole thing can be summarized in just one sentence: 'That is how the heart is.'

The lesson here is that while making dosas, french fries, or pizza it is important to be a good cook. When you are with your children, be a good father or mother. When you speak, be a good speaker, but when others speak, allow them to speak and be a good listener as well. And when you are in the office, be a superb manager. Look into the management at the micro and macro level. There is nothing new, superhuman, or miraculous in this. This is just how life should be managed. And this is exactly what Amma does.

A wealthy man came to see a great master. There was a garden in front of the master's cottage, where he saw a man engaged in gardening. The wealthy man asked him, "May I know who you are?"

"It's obvious, isn't it? I'm a gardener," he replied.

The wealthy man said, "I see that. I am here to see your master."

"Which master? I don't have one."

The rich man thought it was useless talking to this person. However, to finish the dialogue he asked the man in the garden, "But you own this place, don't you?"

"Perhaps," was his response.

The wealthy man came in. The cottage was a little far away from the gate. The front door of the house was open. There, inside the house, was the gardener sitting in a calm and composed mood.

The surprised rich man asked, "Aren't you the same person I met at the front gate, or are you his twin brother?"

"Maybe," said the 'gardener.'

The wealthy man said, "Who is that person doing gardening?"

"Who else, but a gardener."

Seeing the predicament of the wealthy man, the master said, "No need to be confused. You did not see two identical people. It was the same person doing two different jobs. I am a gardener when I doing gardening, and I am a master when I teach my students. I sometimes play golf. At that time, I am a perfect golfer. Whatever I do, I become that."

This is exactly what it means when Amma says, "Awaken the child within." A child always remains whole, moving from one moment to another.

When, the pure energy of love awakens the child within you, you never lose your patience. A child who is in the process of learning to walk never gives up. No matter how many times it falls, a child's determination and faith never fails. After each fall, it gains more strength and bounces back into action.

Chapter Twelve

Yet Another "Pyramid of Fortune"

I recently read an article written by Justin Fox, the editorial director of the *Harvard Business Review Group* and business and economics columnist for *Time Magazine*. Though short, the article was tastefully written with a nice flavor. It unfolded like a fable. The author talked about his encounter with the management expert, the late C. K. Prahalad.

A month before CKP died, the author had a get-together with him in New York. As they spoke over lunch, Justin Fox jotted down a summary of the ideas CKP shared with him. One day when the writer was cleaning out his backpack after the demise of the management expert, he found several pages of scribbling from their lunch conversation buried in his backpack. The author of the article, Justin Fox, recaptured CK Prahalad's thoughts in the following words:

"In the 1850s, a sewing machine cost more than US$100. With the average American family taking in about US$500 a year, that price put it out of reach for most. Then, in 1856, the I.M. Singer Company introduced an installment plan through which buyers could pay for its machines over time. Sales tripled in the first year. Singer became the first U.S. Company to make it big globally, and its installment-plan customers saw their lives improved and enriched. He wrapped it up with the aphorism: "If you build it for the poor, the rich can come. If you build it for the rich, the poor can't come." That's what he calls, 'Fortune at the Bottom of the Pyramid,' an innovative business-model. In essence, the business model he presented was, 'generate money by providing for the world's neediest.' Reminiscent of Prahalad's book, '*The Fortune at the Bottom of the Pyramid*,' Justin Fox's article is titled, '*The Fortune at the Bottom of my Backpack*.' The title of the article was a play on Prahalad's book title and was indicative of the value of the scribbled notes the writer found buried in his backpack.

How correct is the expert's statement regarding the importance of building for the poor so that the rich can come?

Amma has a very different perspective. She transforms the rich, so that they can serve the poor. Amma says, "If the rich people in our world develop a compassionate outlook, it will highly benefit the poor. Since the rich own immense wealth and the required resources, they certainly will be willing to help the suffering people, provided they transform." Amma creates this transformation in the 'haves' and through them she helps the 'have nots.'

Amma says, "There are two types of poverty in the world. One is the poverty of love and compassion. The other is the poverty of clothing, food, and shelter. If we develop love and compassion, then we will naturally start giving others food, shelter, clothing, etc. and thereby save them. Therefore, poverty of love is the greatest enemy and must be done away with." Amma's main purpose of interacting with people and embracing them is to awaken the pure love and compassion within them.

Based on the findings of the ancient sages, Amma, too, has a 'Fortune Pyramid' model to offer. This pyramid ascends to a much higher level of 'fortune,' a wealth that gives inner richness, which any amount of external fortune fails to provide. An extraordinary feature of this consummate model is that it gives us immeasurable joy and contentment even if we own nothing. Another great advantage of acquiring this 'fortune' is that it transforms both our successes and failures into moments of celebration.

Don't misunderstand and think that this model will lead to losses, failures, and bankruptcy. It will not. Instead, it will take us to both material and spiritual heights.

There is a 'fortune' at the bottom of this 'pyramid' model as well. Amma says, "Just like a pyramid, human life has four sides: *dharma, artha, kama* and *moksha*—the pursuit of virtue, the pursuit of money, the pursuit of pleasure, and the pursuit of liberation." These four comprise the very foundation stones of life. They are vital for the survival of an individual. Make money and enjoy pleasures, but do it in accordance with the law of the universe, dharma. Be in harmony with that law. This will lead you to lasting happiness and complete freedom. Compare the two models. You will find the one recommended by the ancient seers far superior, because along with the material gains we achieve, we also attain an unperturbed and peaceful state of mind.

Mr. Ron Gottsegen was a successful and well-established American businessman when he met Amma in 1987 during her first visit to the United States. He was the founder of a public company by the name of *Radionics* that manufactured digital alarm systems. In fact, he was the inventor of the first programmable electronic security system. In his own words, "I had already fulfilled a need to prove myself on my own - away from family and independent. Business was no longer a challenge. Financial success had come rather quickly and easily for me although that was not my goal, and financial success did not change my life style. I had sought creative expression in the process of building a quality company that was a recognized industry leader. Romantic relationships were never satisfactory and always a source of discomfort to the point I preferred my solitude. But I was not emotionally mature, as I never understood my true nature. I had been divorced about 15 years and had been the primary caregiver to two boys from the ages of 11 and 13."

Meeting Amma was the beginning of a great transformation for Ron. His life gradually unfolded until he reached a point of realization. He says, "I suppose that my destiny had been preordained, but I feel those first 40 years of my life brought me to the point of understanding that the conventional material values and trappings of life held no luster."

It is best to put the rest of the story in Ron's own words, "I was never able to penetrate deeply into a greater understanding of things, heal the old wounds from mental consciousness, nor to reset the habitual patterns of mind and action to a grounded state of centered calm. But over the next 26 years of my relationship with Amma, I was able to deepen my understanding, break old patterns, and reinforce the good ones. Most importantly, it has been the loving service to Amma's causes that has been the most transforming as that deepens my intuition and allows wisdom to manifest. As my faith and conviction became more solid, my inner strength grew to an eventual joyful state. This is a very productive period for me personally. I do not know what lies ahead, but it does not matter as I tangibly feel that I am in the flow. I will be forever grateful for what I have and am still receiving."

Our hankering to earn more and more money, this insatiable craving, is a sign of our inner and subtler desire to become expansive. Though it is expressed as our desire to acquire wealth, in reality it is indicative of our Self's nature, which is happiness itself. We are searching for happiness outside, but happiness is actually inside. Thus, we will never be truly happy with the material achievements we gain.

Money and happiness can co-exist together peacefully. None of the religious texts, the scriptures, were ever against money. This concept is vividly elaborated in one of the major Upanishads, *Taittiriya Upanishad*. The text talks about gaining four things: obtaining Wealth, Purity of Mind, Knowledge, and Students.

Even though wealth is listed first in the list, the Upanishad says, "After that, bring me *Lakshmi Devi* (The Goddess of Prosperity)." The word, 'after' has an implied meaning: "after gaining wisdom." Money should come only after gaining knowledge of dharma—the code of righteousness—otherwise, it will lead one to ruin and evil. A major problem, especially in rich countries, is that people don't know what to use money for and what not to use money for. This scripture gives clear guidance on that matter.

There is significance to the above order. First, obtain wealth because money is required to live and perform action in our designated area. So the request regarding wealth is to use it for the well being of society. However, we should gain right understanding, wisdom, on how to use the money for the right purposes. When we use wealth selflessly—for the betterment of society—it leads to a pure mind. With that pure mind, we should obtain true knowledge about life, the higher goal of life. And then, finally, we should teach others to preserve the tradition of righteousness, dharma.

Knowledge of dharma is what makes Amma a distinct leader. Her policy is, 'Give every single penny we receive back to society. Return it with maximum interest. This keeps us always full.' She is true to her teachings. Even her physical body has become an offering to society. In her own words, "The body will perish one day. So, rather than becoming rusty without doing any good work for the uplift of society, I prefer to wear out offering myself to the world. The greatest tragedy is not death; it is the capacities within us rusting from our not using them. Since everything is a gift from the universe, we cannot really claim anything. At best, we can offer it back to the universe so that our body, mind, intellect, and wealth becomes a good tool to serve humanity as a whole."

The late Ms. Yolanda King, daughter of Martin Luther King, Jr. and Director, *Martin Luther King, Jr. Center* (USA) was a great admirer of Amma. The following is her perception of Amma, "What I cherish most about Amma is that she not only talks the talk and is an embodiment of unconditional love, but she expresses that love in action. She walks the talk! Amma is the change she wishes to see in our world."

Chapter Thirteen

The Power of Reverence

"Just as a fire is covered by smoke and a mirror is obscured by dust, just as the embryo rests deep within the womb, wisdom is hidden by selfish desire."

—Bhagavad Gita

"Neither fire, nor moisture, nor wind can destroy the blessing of good deeds, and blessings enlighten the whole world."

—Buddha

Some people are remembered for their cruelty and inhuman activities while others are remembered for their unshakeable courage and patriotism. A handful are remembered for setting an example of good leadership qualities. But rare are those who are remembered as a guiding light to the world, for the virtuous circle they continue to create, their fearless attitude, and their undivided love for humanity. Neither humans, nor the passing of time can destroy their fame and splendidness.

As the Bhagavad Gita rightly puts it,

"He who is of the same mind to the good-hearted, friends, enemies, the indifferent, the neutral, the hateful, the relatives, the righteous and the unrighteous, excels."

Creating a lasting impact in the hearts of people and leaving a legacy of respect and inspiration for generations to come is not a path strewn with flowers. Had it been an easy path to walk, numerous people would have happily meandered along it. But this path is an austere way of life. More than successful and happy moments, one is confronted with failures and criticisms. Mediocre minds will never understand such broadminded and forgiving people. These shining examples have always been put through humiliating situations. But their convictions about life and the value system they follow are as firm and unflinching as a mighty mountain. As such, every single challenge they have to face deepens their faith and fortifies their actions, which enables them to fulfill the mission they have undertaken.

Amma says, "Education, acquisition of knowledge, science and technology may help us advance to unimaginable levels, but if the result is a mentally and emotionally immature generation with no sense of discrimination and respect, it would be truly catastrophic. If you ask me, 'Which is more important, rights or respect?' I would say, 'Claiming rights respectfully is what is most important.' Asserting one's rights without being respectful of others will only succeed in increasing our ego. If we claim our rights respectfully, then our love, understanding, and trust will build a bridge to other people. When we approach others with respect that is firmly established in a deep understanding and acceptance of each other's differences, then our communications will truly become dialogues."

In 2001, an earthquake devastated Western Gujarat in India. Twenty-thousand people died, and most of the survivors lost their homes. Our NGO responded by adopting three villages in a remote area called Bhuj. When we arrived, the people were fearful that we would try to influence their culture, religion, and lifestyle. We patiently explained that we wanted to rebuild their villages exactly as they wished. We ended up building 1200 houses for the victims as well as temples, mosques, churches, and other halls of worship.

Three years later, during the 2004 tsunami in southern Asia, the area surrounding our NGO headquarters on the Arabian Sea was flooded. As soon as the people from Bhuj heard, hundreds of them put aside all differences of culture and religion and rushed to help us aid the victims. When journalists asked them why they had made the long journey from the North to the South of India, they replied, "When we faced suffering and loss, Amma's NGO did not try to change our culture, religion, or way of life. They compassionately gave us what we requested. We are forever indebted."

Compared to Kerala, these people have completely different traditions, food habits, and lifestyle patterns. The fact that our NGO respected and recognized their traditions inspired them to wholeheartedly give back to society in a similar manner. Since then, whenever there has been any natural disaster in India, these villagers from Bhuj arrive on the scene to help our volunteers.

We have had similar experiences with some of the tribal groups in Kerala and other states. Volunteers from our NGO went into these tribal villages, lived with them, and gained their trust. We were also able to understand their problems and help them find solutions. They were so touched that we would help them while respecting their way of life that they, too, wanted to give back to society and have begun to grow extra vegetables to feed the poor.

Let me quote Amma again, "It is not enough to give a diabetic patient insulin alone. They also need to learn how to eat properly and exercise in order to keep their blood sugar under control.

Similarly, though governments are striving to reduce poverty, it is not enough to focus only on the physical needs of food, money and shelter. We also need to give importance to nourishing the spirit. The food for the soul is love. Where there is love, there is reverence. The cause for 90% of problems in today's world is the lack of love, compassion and forgiveness. Just as the body needs food to grow, the soul requires love to grow and unfold. From such love a reverential attitude ensues. This alone is our hope for the future."

An ancient scriptural saying goes like this,

> *Matru Devo Bhava, Pitru Devo Bhava,*
> *Acharya Devo Bhava, Athithi Devo Bhava.*
>
> *Regard the mother as God, regard the father as God,*
> *regard the teacher as God, and regard the guest as God.*

Some of the private airlines in India address their passengers as 'guests,' which sets a hospitable tone of welcome. When we invite guests to our house, it is part of hospitality to treat them with love and respect, right? Now imagine this. No matter if we run our business from a rented office building or our own building, it is our place. Even though the employees working in that building are paid, aren't they actually our guests? We have invited them, though the invitation in this context is known as an 'appointment letter.' If we view the situation from this angle, shouldn't we be treating all our employees with respect and love as a part of the job? I'm not suggesting that entertainment, merrymaking, and get together parties should be organized on a daily basis and owners of companies should hold heart-to-heart interactive sessions with their managers and employees every day. My point is, instead of seeing our team members only as paid and skilled workers, we should try to value their presence in the company. Whenever an opportunity comes, express gratitude for having them on the team with a big hearty smile and a few gentle words of appreciation. A loving enquiry about their family can create a big impact.

I see this in a larger scale in Amma's life. Even in a huge crowd of people, I have witnessed the concern Amma expresses about the crowd in general, and sick and elderly people in particular. Soon after she begins her personal interaction with each person gathered at a program, Amma's first question to the people working close to her will be, "Did you make sure that elderly and sick people in the crowd are well taken care of? Instruct the volunteers to bring them on a priority basis. Feed them and ask their relatives to give medicines to them at the right time, particularly if they are diabetic or high blood pressure patients. Mothers with little children should also be given preference." Most of the time, she, herself, picks up the microphone and makes these announcements. Also, when it is too warm during the day or too cold during the night, Amma immediately issues instructions to cover the area to shield it from the sun or to turn on heat lamps if it is too cold.

Former CEO and President, Jim Sinegal, who founded *Costco* and turned it into the third largest retailer in the U.S. before he retired, was well known for his fair treatment of employees. He created a model that rewards workers handsomely even while competitors were cutting benefits. Costco is renowned for offering above-average pay for warehouse-store workers. The result is low turnover, low training costs, and a family feeling in the company. They don't have to do much recruiting, as current employees are happy to put out the word to family and friends. Eighty-six percent of the employees have healthcare and benefits, even though half are part-timers, and the average wage is $19 an hour. And Costco didn't have any layoffs in the recession. "It's really pretty simple. It's good business. When you hire good people, and you provide good jobs and good wages and a career, good things are going to happen," Sinegal says. "We try to give a message of quality in everything that we do, and we think that that starts with the people. It doesn't do much good to have a quality image, whether it's with the facility or whether it's with the merchandise, if you don't have real quality people taking care of your customers."

Sinegal was a good example of humility. His office was in the hallway at Costco's Issaquah headquarters in the state of Washington. He didn't have a door that shut. Not even a glass wall between him and the rest of the staff. Anybody could wander by and chat with him, anytime. He also freely gave out his cell phone number, whereas most executives would make people call a secretary and have that person patch the call through. There were no layers of handlers around Sinegal. Despite commanding a US$76 billion retail empire, he was honest, straightforward, and down-to-earth. His desk was a cheap, Formica-topped folding table (a sale item from Costco). Nothing fancy for this man. But maybe most importantly, because he valued his employees and customers so much, he was constantly listening to their comments on how he could serve them.

With regard to time management, how can we, in today's busy life, find the time to show genuine respect and caring to everyone we work with? Amma is one of the busiest people in the world. She works seven days a week, 365 days a year. She works around the clock without taking a single day off. And even after sitting for hours meeting people, at night when she retires to her room, she still finds time to read all the letters, to give a personal call to her volunteers working on various humanitarian activities, and to plan and discuss new projects.

Maturity has nothing to do with age. However, there is big difference between old age and aging. Old age happens only when we resolve and dissolve the accumulated hard feelings with others through proper contemplation. Spend some time every day recalling any hurt feelings or unhealed wounds caused by someone close to you, or otherwise. Mentally visualize that person and imagine you are holding a beautifully fragrant rose flower. Then imagine that the beauty of the flower fills your heart and soul. With a prayer, "May my life open up like this flower," offer the flower to them and say, "I forgive you. Please forgive me, if I have done anything wrong to you."

Wisdom arises gradually when we win over the negative emotions by assimilating them. This rising up and above the past is known as old age. That is when we attain maturity. If this transition does not take place, then it is only aging. However, it is foolish to wait that long for wisdom and maturity to evolve. It can occur at a much earlier stage in life if the desire is there. As Amma says, "Just as we go to school from kindergarten on and like we eat and sleep, imbibing and practicing values should become a part and parcel of our life."

Only a mature leader will be able to show respect to his team and love them. So, respect and genuine concern are the two main qualities that a good leader should have. Many young leaders and managers have brilliant ideas. They have unbelievable liveliness and enthusiasm. They have the skill to change the world. But they should also have respect for others. Unfortunately, disrespect is the hallmark of many youth.

Amma says, "In reality, youth is the center-point of life. They are neither a child nor a grownup. Youngsters have unimaginable energy. If channelled properly, they can train their mind as needed, thereby tapping into the infinite energy that is available in the present moment. Sadly, the face of human life called youth is disappearing. In today's world, people go from childhood straight to old age without maturing. This lack of maturity blocks the development of love and respect."

Shel Silverstein, author-artist, cartoonist, playwright, poet, performer, recording artist, and Grammy-winning, Oscar-nominated songwriter's short and beautiful poem:

'The Little Boy and the Old Man'

Said the little boy, "Sometimes I drop my spoon."
Said the old man, "I do that too."
The little boy whispered, "I wet my pants."
"I do that too," laughed the little old man.
Said the little boy, "I often cry."
The old man nodded, "So do I."
"But worst of all," said the boy, "it seems
Grown-ups don't pay attention to me."
And he felt the warmth of a wrinkled old hand.
"I know what you mean," said the little old man.

Chapter Fourteen

Ahimsa in Action

"The whole world is divided for me into two parts: one is she, and there is all happiness, hope, light; the other is where she is not, and there is dejection and darkness..."

—Leo Tolstoy, *War and Peace*

My interpretation of Leo Tolstoy's words is, "one is she" refers to the feminine and "where she is not" is the masculine. It is almost like the *Ardhanareeswara* (half God and half Goddess, the male and female energies, the *yin* and *yang*) image in the Hindu faith.

War and peace is the nature of the world from an objective point of view. If there is no external conflict, there is internal conflict. Internal conflict manifests external conflict. It is a vicious circle. To become an extreme practitioner of *ahimsa* (non-violence) is impractical. What we actually need is achievable non-violence. It is such a profound principle, but is there a way to translate this elegant virtue into action without impeding our activities in the world? We don't want people to say, "The idea is good but not practical."

I would say Lord Krishna practiced the most sensible form of ahimsa. The war waged at the Kurukshetra battlefield did not arise through his choice, or through the choice of the Pandava brothers. Duryodhana and his brothers, counseled and conditioned by their physically and mentally blind father and their evil-minded uncle, Sakuni, hold the sole responsibility for the war. Scheming as they were, using crooked methods, they snatched everything that rightfully belonged to the Pandavas. They drove the Pandavas out of the country and even tried to kill the five righteous brothers multiple times.

When the Pandava brothers returned after spending thirteen long years in the forest, they were ruthlessly denied their kingdom and other privileges. Krishna tried his best to establish peace between them and thus avert a war and the ensuing massive destruction. However, all his efforts utterly failed when the wicked Duryodhana arrogantly proclaimed, "I can sacrifice my life, my wealth, my kingdom, my everything, but I can never live in peace with the Pandavas. I will not surrender to them even as much land as can be pierced by the point of a needle." He made excuses for his nature, "I am whatever the gods have made me." Thus he slammed shut all the doors to peace and mercilessly chose war. Regardless of one's wealth, power, arrogance and knowledge, everyone will have to reap the result of their actions, and Duryodhana surely did through his own merciless death.

Do we have a choice but to fight when being denied what lawfully belongs to us? Or when someone is bent on destroying us? Or determined to throw us out in the streets? Or denying us even the right to live? Whether it happened 5,000 years ago or in the present day world, if you are abused from all directions, what else can you do but fight for your rights? No one with self-respect, whether an individual, a nation, or any of the countries of our international community would ever recoil from such a situation.

The *Mahabharata* gives a powerful and practical description of a real life situation. Krishna's advice to Arjuna in the Bhagavad Gita on the need to discharge his duties as a warrior took place in the midst of the din and roar of the battlefield. Nowhere else in the history of mankind will we find such a shining example of calm in the midst of chaos.

The Mahabharata war was about to begin. All of a sudden, overcome by grief born out of intense emotional attachment, Arjuna put his bow and arrow down and refused to fight. Remember, whether or not Arjuna chose to fight, the enemies were determined to wipe out Arjuna, his brothers, and the entire race. Overwhelmed, he became delirious and deluded. Instead of discharging his duty to protect his people and the kingdom, he was engaged in philosophizing. In this time of extreme crisis, Krishna had the seemingly impossible task of helping Arjuna rise above the situation, of instilling faith and courage in him to fight and win the war. Our lives are full of challenges in our various areas of activity that can lead us to experience despair similar to what Arjuna faced. Therefore, it is important to have a leader like Krishna.

Ahimsa of course means not to harm anyone by word or deed. Ahimsa is to refrain from hurting anyone consciously and includes having a non-violent attitude toward your own self. Some interpret even picking a fruit from a tree as *himsa*, violence. If so, eating a ripe fruit that has fallen from a tree can also be himsa because there are so many fruits and vegetables where we eat the seeds as well. When you eat the seeds, are we not destroying or harming all the plants that might have grown from them? Though not consciously, don't we kill innumerable living beings when we walk, talk, breathe, drink or eat?

Free days are rare when we are with Amma. Be it in our headquarters in Kerala or travelling to other parts of the world, it is Amma's policy to give the maximum to people. This has been

Amma's practice for the last 40 years. This incident happened a few years ago when we were in Switzerland. It was one of those special occasions of enjoying a free day. That evening Amma went for a stroll. A few of us accompanied her. At one point we all sat near an apple grove. The owner of the apple grove was also with us.

It was a pleasant evening, clear and sunny. Surrounded by nature's abundance and inhaling the pure air, we sat there experiencing the inner silence. Approximately half an hour passed like this. Thereafter, a short conversation ensued when someone asked Amma whether there was a solution for the current problems in the world. Amma said, "In one word, 'love.' In two, 'love and compassion.' With these two, if you add one more 'patience,' we can solve all the major problems in the world. Allow these qualities to have a predominant influence in your life. In reality, it is enough to practice one of these qualities, all others will follow."

When we were about to get up and leave, Amma suddenly wanted to give something to everyone. Since we did not have anything else, someone suggested Amma pick a few apples and distribute them to everyone. Amma got up from her seat and walked up to one of the apple trees. She gently and lovingly touched and caressed the tree first. Then with her palms joined, she bowed down to the tree and uttered these words, "Please forgive me and allow me to pick a few apples..." She waited a few seconds as if waiting for the permission of the tree and then gently plucked a few well-ripened fruit. Before she returned to her seat, Amma once again bowed down to the tree.

Before leaving, Amma took some flower petals and worshipped the tree and took a water bottle from a member of the group and poured some water at the foot of the tree saying, "Your willingness to share everything with others makes you so beautiful.

May your example be remembered, and may those who come to you feel inspired by it." In one of Amma's talks, she mentioned, "Protecting, preserving, and above all, worshipping nature, was part of many ancient cultures. What we lack is reverence, a unique compassionate outlook that our ancestors had toward all forms of life. This is a major reason that our attempts at nature preservation are not always successful."

True ahimsa is the overflow of love as compassionate action. We have visionaries in almost all areas of knowledge. What we truly lack are people who have a 'visionary perspective' towards life, a sense of a larger vision in one's work for the common good.

Compassionate leadership doesn't imply: 'Take no action. Keep your mouth shut and swallow all humiliations and unfair deeds done to you or others.' Rather, it is a fearless attitude, an extraordinary aptitude to remain alert and mentally awake in all situations of life. The light of right judgment, discrimination, and maturity never leaves a compassionate leader.

In the beginning, when Amma initially began to receive people by embracing everyone who came to see her, there was a lot of protest and disapproval from her own family members. From one angle, their disapproval was understandable because a young girl hugging people of all ages, regardless of gender, was not at all part of the culture. They feared that it would bring disgrace and irreversible damage to the whole family, including all the relatives. One of their major concerns was that nobody from a reputable family would come forward with a marriage proposal for the girls in the family.

When all their efforts failed to stop Amma from continuing her 'strange behavior,' one of her cousins locked her in a room and raised a knife, threatening to take her life if she did not stop her way of embracing people. Amma was unperturbed and did not budge even an inch in yielding to his request. She calmly told him, "Kill me if you wish to. But come what may, I'm not going to change my ways under any circumstance. I want to offer my life to the world, comfort and console the suffering people, until I breathe my last. I completely surrender myself to this cause." As Mahatma Gandhi rightly observed, "A 'No' uttered from the deepest conviction is better than a 'Yes' merely uttered to please, or worse, to avoid trouble."

Whoever it may be, when someone is unwaveringly courageous and fearless like this, even when death stares at them, the person who is ready to victimize them, no matter how vicious he is, will suddenly feel weak and disarmed. Having witnessed Amma's power of will and the firmness in her words, the cousin was shocked and left the room in utter desperation.

Months later when he fell sick, Amma visited him in the hospital. She sat next to him, fed him, and spoke kind words to him. He was full of remorse. Amma's visit and the loving words she shared with him helped him to open up. The man confessed his mistake and apologized to her. Amma made him feel happy and peaceful. Only a fearless person can forgive, and a forgiving person will always be fearless. Frankly, no one can be a good leader unless he or she is capable of forgiving. Forgiveness is forgetting the past.

We see a unique example of forgiveness and fearlessness in this incident. Thus, if the leader is like a powerful light that illuminates an entire city, the followers will strive, at least, to be like a candle.

During the 2004 tsunami, Amma proved herself to be completely fearless person. During the tsunami, when even adept swimmers and fishermen who frequently go into the deep seas seemed to be gripped by fear, Amma charged right down into the floodwaters. Another wave could have come at any moment, but Amma was not concerned about herself in the least. She was only concerned about the people.

"Let us not pray to be sheltered from dangers but to be fearless when facing them."

—Rabindranath Tagore

Chapter Fifteen

Aggressiveness Versus Assertiveness

The condition of our world would not be as calamitous as it is today if our grandparents had been wise enough to make the right decisions. We are reaping the result of their actions in addition to the fruit of our own mistakes. That said, we should also remember that whatever we do now is definitely going to affect future generations. Obviously, we are not setting a good example. Many of us cannot help but wonder, 'What could be in store for future generations, for our children and grandchildren?'

Our mad arrogance has already done irreparable damage to nature and humanity as a whole. Wherever we go, we will find people with, 'I'm the chosen one' attitude. A newly recruited police officer, a freshly appointed young manager, professionals, artists, laborers and even among spiritual seekers and religious leaders, there is no scarcity in finding people with a 'Who are you to teach me?' attitude.

In my observation of people's behavior, there are three types of egoistic people in this world: extremely egoistic people, diplomatically egoistic people, and humbly, or subtly, egoistic people. It is easy to recognize extremely egoistic people. They simply express it. It is their nature. You can't do much about it, but you can definitely take some precautionary measures. It isn't difficult to recognize the diplomatically egoistic people either. Just beneath the surface, we can see their ego ready to take a leap.

However, the humbly egoistic people are not easily detectable. Almost always they wear a mask that prevents them from being caught. Their communication style, choice of words, tone, and external appearance carry brimming humbleness, which is very deceptive. Such characters are far more dangerous than those who bluntly express their ego. Moreover, often their ego is subtle but of greater intensity than the other two groups.

Amma says, "Arrogance is like the morning flower. Head up with pride, it stays on the plant announcing to the world, 'Look at me. See my beauty. I'm the best among creation.' However, by sunset, it's completely beaten up, exhausted and with no claims, the flower remains with its head hung down, before it falls off the plant."

A person's character is inbuilt into the system. Some of these strong tendencies, behavioral patterns, and habits are born with the person and others are developed or cultivated. To put it in scientific terms, 'It is in the person's genes.' Such being the situation, nothing much can be done about it by an outside source. The correction has to be done from inside.

Peter Drucker says, "To be able to manage yourself, you finally have to ask, 'what are my values?' Ethics requires that you ask yourself, 'What kind of person do I want to see in the mirror in the morning?'"

The fact is that many competent managers have a weakness of being indiscriminately arrogant. What makes it really challenging is that the person does a self-evaluation and sees his arrogant attitude as a plus rather than a minus. A manager incapable of controlling his or her arrogance often misses many wonderful opportunities.

I have seen the way Amma handles people of this mental makeup. A few years ago, when we were at the airport in Detroit, Michigan, I met a man at the airport lounge. He was with his family. He worked as a senior manager in one of the multinational companies in Detroit. Along with his family, the man was on his way to Kerala, India, where he was born and brought up. He and I had a rather lengthy conversation though we had never met before. Actually, it was a monologue as he did most of the talking. As his story unfolded, he proudly and repeatedly emphasized his atheistic point of view. From the frequent voicing of his unshakeable stance as an atheist, I felt that he wasn't really convinced about his beliefs. To be honest, the more he spoke, the more judgmental I became. It reached a point where I could no longer stand his false pride and arrogant statements. I was reminded of Albert Einstein's quote, "What separates me from most so-called atheists is a feeling of utter humility and reverence toward the unattainable secrets of the harmony of the cosmos."

As we were conversing, Amma entered the lounge. A unique feature of Amma's personality is that whether she is in another country or with people from a different culture, no situation is strange to her. Hence her entry had absolutely no air of self-importance. As always, it was simple and natural.

As soon as my 'atheist friend' saw Amma enter, the grin on his face vanished. Standing next to him, I could see the man's body language change and could feel the unwelcoming vibes emanating from him. He quickly stepped backwards, but Amma was quicker. With a smiling face, she placed her hands on the man's shoulder and asked, "Are you from Kerala?"

He looked at me. I smiled at him. When someone you consider, 'strange or weird' expresses acceptance of you with a natural ease, it is difficult to remain tight-lipped. It is like when a child smiles at us. We cannot help but smile back even if it is the child of our enemy. The man seemed a little stunned at Amma's 'unusual behavior.' He had to say, "Yes, I am" to Amma's question. This was followed by another query, "Are you from Trissur?"

The man was obviously surprised that Amma could recognize his native town, and his answer came in the form of a question, "How did you know?"

"Your accent," Amma replied.

"How long have you been here in the US?"

"Just five years."

By then, his wife and two children came close to us. Amma smiled at them and asked the man, "Your family?"

"Yes."

Amma called the little girls near her. She hugged and kissed them on their cheeks. Seeing this, the wife spontaneously placed her head on Amma's shoulder. She, too, received a warm embrace.

The man looked at me, but his eyes weren't the same as those that had initially met me. There was a tinge of sparkle. To cut a long story short, until he and his family left the lounge to board their flight, they all sat next to Amma. Before leaving the room, he, too, wanted to experience Amma's embrace.

The man ended up removing the false mask he had been wearing up to that point and turned out to be an interested and focused listener to what Amma had to say. However, before that, Amma intently and patiently listened to his atheistic beliefs, his family background, and his past associations.

Only when he had finished talking did Amma say, "I agree with what you have said, but no matter what your beliefs are, if you have empathy for the less fortunate ones, if you have the willingness to lend a helping hand to the poor and needy, I really admire that person. It is okay to have political inclinations. Be an atheist, but be humane and have faith in human values. Just as all genuine political parties, spirituality also believes in serving our fellow humans, the poor and downtrodden. It is almost impossible to refrain from committing mistakes. However, may our inclinations and stances do minimum harm to us and society and maximum benefit for both."

There was a sudden change in the man's attitude. He certainly looked different. The tightness was gone. As he was leaving the room, he told me, "Meeting her was truly an experience. I'm so impressed by her simplicity and non-judgmental attitude. In fact, I am the one who judged her. Sorry about that. We will certainly meet again."

I'm not sure if this change will have a lasting impact. The point is that the meeting had a powerful effect on this man, which could be the beginning of a new chapter in his life. For this to happen, first Amma had to have an open and non-judgmental approach.

I have witnessed Amma conversing with similar-minded people who are often intellectual thinkers, scientists, or non-believers. She listens to every bit of what they have to say. Only when they are done expressing their views, Amma speaks. And she mostly begins by saying, "What you said is correct. I agree, but..." Then she shares her views on the topic.

This is an immensely effective approach that any professional can experiment with. Actually, this technique works wonders. Be patient and let the other person feel how genuinely interested you are in listening. People effortlessly open up in front of Amma because they get the feeling that, 'Here is someone who values my opinions and observations. She is the right person to communicate and work with. She understands me.'

Talk to any one of the professionals working at Amma's institutions or the large number of volunteers serving the NGO's massive humanitarian undertakings. Listen to their stories. There is one single thread that strings the whole group of people together: their personal bond with their leader. I am reminded of Amma's quote: "Love is our true essence. Love has no limitations of caste, religion, race or nationality. We are all *beads* strung together on the *same thread* of love." Since love is the main ingredient, the connection is spontaneous. The unfolding of the relationship is natural, so natural that each person reaches a point when they realize, 'This is what I want. This companionship will nourish my soul and heal my body and mind.'

I still wonder how it is possible for Amma to attract these professionals from all walks of life from across the globe to work for her, to serve the organization. It remains as an unanswered question for me, but I do see that although these individuals are not seeking name and fame, they now have opportunities they would not have had if they had remained in their respective positions and countries. In the name of *Amrita*, in the name of Amma, they now have connections with experts all over the world, and they are actually becoming well known in their Amrita roles.

They also see that Amma is fair to the core; that she has no ulterior motives. People get a direct and tangible experience of her one and only goal as selflessly serving society through an equal distribution of wealth, the inner wealth of love and compassion and the outer wealth of resources. So, their decision to join hands with her is effortless and without any apprehensions.

I don't mean to say that there are no problems. Glitches are there. They raise their heads every now and then, but there is always a solution. The problems are mostly resolved through a simple, informal meeting or conversation. Above all, if required, Amma is always accessible, at any time of the day or night, as a powerful catalyst, a medium connecting every one of us. Every single individual in our organization, regardless of his or her status or designation, spontaneously connects with Amma. Whatever problem arises, taking it to Amma means it ends there. That is the limit, no going beyond.

Amma is the Chancellor of Amrita University, perhaps the one and only Chancellor accessible to anyone and everyone. All complaints, requests, problems, whether they are personal or professional, can be directly submitted to her.

When it is necessary, Amma is assertive. However, she is neither aggressive nor arrogant. Aggressiveness and assertiveness are two different mental states. In our daily interactions with the world, we hear people say, "I was just being assertive." Taking a closer look, we realize that in truth, they were belligerent and aggressive, not assertive.

An aggressive behavior normally will have a hidden agenda, a personal goal to fulfill. It shows self-importance rather than self-confidence. Assertiveness is a trait illustrating a person's self-confidence, born out of experience. In other words, an aggressive attitude is the outward expression of an immature ego. On the contrary, assertiveness is a more matured ego. Aggressiveness is predominantly an unreceptive and unfriendly attitude. Assertiveness is a cultured and graceful mindset. There is a huge difference between the two. The former has little consideration for others,

'Whatever the goal, I want to win and gain. I don't care whether you get anything or not, period.'

On the other hand, an assertive individual politely considers the opinions and views of other people. This perception manifests in varied forms such as low, medium, and high intensity levels. Similarly, depending on the person's maturity and understanding, aggressiveness, too, has minimum, mediocre and maximum intensity levels.

In my experience, Amma is a unique leader who is tactfully firm and assertive as well as compassionately receptive. I would say that she is 'hard as a diamond and soft as a flower.' She flows like a river and stands like a mountain. She has a special skill, beyond compare, to establish contact with people externally and internally. Regarding her hugs, Amma says, "It is not just a physical hug where only two bodies meet; it is a real meeting of hearts." That heart to heart communication is the key to establishing contact.

We rarely see Amma in a forceful mood. But when a disaster hits, when things are critical, Amma intensifies her energy outflow. In that moment, Amma lets her assertive energy take over. It should be pointed out, though, that Amma controls the speed, never allowing the energy of aggressiveness to come into play and overpower her or her team.

For me and for thousands of people who serve society under Amma's leadership from around the world, these 'high-energy level action scenarios' keep us steeped in waves of positive vibrations and tremendous inspiration. It would be unrealistic to say that these situations are completely free of tension. However, even in the midst of such wild undertakings, Amma is capable of creating a sense of deep satisfaction and exuberance in the hearts of her team members. People work out of inspiration and love, not out of force or fear. As such, even though the body feels tired, the mind and the enthusiasm level are ablaze.

Amma has various ways of managing any situation. Depending on the circumstances and the disposition, as well as the culture and character of the people involved, she adopts a plan that is most suitable to finish the work cost-effectively, proficiently, and within the shortest possible time. Unlike other occasions when Amma initiates detailed discussions, periods of crisis and disaster are managed and handled in an entirely different way. Amma takes sole control of the situation. Every single instruction comes from her, and she tirelessly leads the planning and implementation, foregoing food and sleep. She is adept at high, medium and low speed management systems. She also knows when to put her foot down.

After the Karnataka (Raichur) floods of 2009, our NGO pledged to construct 2000 houses as part of the rehabilitation process.

On November 27th, the MAM announced a Relief and Rehabilitation package of Rs.50 crores (US$10.7 million) for those affected by the floods. Amma sent a team to survey the devastation. They brought back the name of one village, which no aid group had offered to assist. Amma offered to rehabilitate this village. That is how the construction of a thousand houses began in Dongrampura (Raichur District) replete with roads, parks, electricity, water, and a community center.

On January 16th, a team of 14 volunteers landed in Raichur during a solar eclipse. Although according to local tradition one is not supposed to look at the sun or walk outdoors during an eclipse day, the volunteers traversed the area without hesitation, visiting the proposed site and meeting the various district officials. The next day, the paperwork was finalized, and the very same day, the mammoth construction work commenced.

Amma instructed the team, "Finish the work quickly. Super speed…" The team took 'speed' as their mantra. They literally toiled nonstop, though the temperature soared to 45 degrees Celsius (113 degrees Fahrenheit). Half of each day there would be no electricity or running water. Braving these hostile circumstances, the volunteers built the first 100 houses in 20 days. They had fulfilled their leader's dream of providing quick solace to those who were rendered homeless by the floods.

This construction miracle broke all records. Statewide, their accomplishment created waves of awe from the elected officials to the professionals, from the shopkeepers to the educators and students. The government created a PowerPoint presentation of this incredible feat to inspire other NGOs. They came in droves to see with their own eyes. Articles appeared in daily newspapers, heaping praises. Government ministers and top civil servants offered tributes from public platforms.

The Chief Minister of Karnataka shared with everyone how the MAM's involvement with the government came about. "On 15th January the MAM entered into an MOU (memorandum of understanding) with the government. And within 20 days, Amma's organization had completed 100 houses and the keys were handed over to me. I am grateful to Amma. This will inspire other donors to complete projects with the same zeal and urgency."

The keys to 242 additional houses were handed over on August 4, 2010, to the grateful Chief Minister of the state of Karnataka during Amma's Bangalore program. New records were broken again and again. Today, almost all the allotted 1000 houses on the three construction sites stand completed.

Is compassionate leadership superior? I would say 'yes,' because a compassionate leader takes the responsibility of helping others without being asked to do so. They don't have to, but it is their nature, and it cannot be otherwise. They are devoid of self-interest and have no fear in doing what they do for society, for the poor and needy. They are completely free of any ambiguity with regards to their mission in life. Above all, they have no expectations, no vested interest. They simply consider this service as their responsibility. This is how Amma is. She thinks less about herself and more about other living beings. She has an in-depth understanding of life and people's hearts and can effortlessly handle any situation, because she is egoless.

Amma is the type of leader/manager who personally comes out into the field rolling up her sleeves and making herself available to do any type of work. Crossing all barriers, this five foot tall figure of Amma, born and brought up in a remote village in Southern India, has created a revolution in the conventional system. Amma bestows on the world a new, deeper dimension to love, the way it should be expressed, its power to transform, and how vital it is in human life.

Nobody asked Amma to serve society, to help the poor and needy, to sit hours on end and listen to people, to undertake massive humanitarian projects. She does it because it is like her life breath. And she makes us feel that by making small corrections and adjustments, all of us can do the same thing.

"Keep away from people who belittle your ambitions. Small people always do that, but the really great make you feel that you, too, can become great."

—Mark Twain

Chapter Sixteen

Impenetrable Conviction and Instantaneous Decision

"Our human compassion binds us the one to the other – not in pity or patronizingly, but as human beings who have learnt how to turn our common suffering into hope for the future."
—Nelson Mandela

Amma has undertaken massive service activities across India and abroad. However, it is the 2004 South East Asia tsunami that still stands as the most brilliant depiction of Amma's competence and adroitness in action. The entire evacuation, relief, and rehabilitation process was completely managed by Amma without missing a single detail. Her disaster relief process demonstrates how to conscientiously respond to an emergency. It is a great lesson in disaster management, resource management, financial management, time management, intuitive decision-making, and most importantly, managing a large crowd of people.

The 2004 tsunami killed thousands of people in Southern India, Indonesia, Andaman Nicobar Islands and Sri Lanka. Amma's proactive leadership qualities, with her innate touch of compassion and fair dealing, were visible throughout. It took almost two years to complete the entire rehabilitation process.

During this period Amma was not only supervising the tsunami activities of the MAM. She was simultaneously supervising the micro and macro aspects of all the humanitarian and educational projects of her NGO.

It was sudden; in the twinkling of an eye the gigantic waves snatched away everything. First it was the waves receding more than a kilometer into the ocean, a beautiful sight revealing the sparkling white sand that lay beneath the ocean waters. It appeared that the entire seashore was covered with tiny white pearls. Hundreds of residents from our Center and local villagers thronged to witness the wondrous sight. But when Amma heard about this unusual sight, she knew it wasn't a good sign. She ordered everyone to immediately return to the Center and instructed the thousands of people gathered to move to the upper floors of the buildings. In a few minutes time, giant-sized waves rose up, swallowing houses and innocent people, including children and women. Within a moment's time, everything that was there disappeared into oblivion.

Amma immediately stopped seeing people and initiated the evacuation process. Wrapping herself in a yellow shawl, she came down and waded through the floodwaters, giving instructions to the thousands of people including the residents and the villagers who came running to the NGO headquarters hoping to find a safe haven. It was a scene of all-consuming panic and utter confusion. Mothers with babies, small boys and girls looking for their parents, the elderly, sick, disabled…it seemed overwhelming and unmanageable.

In a situation like that, when people are in a state of unmitigated bewilderment, only a 'one-[wo]man show,' intelligently handled by a level-headed person will work. The proverb, "Too many cooks spoil the broth," would be a perfect quote for a situation like this. From a management perspective, we may brand this as 'autocratic or authoritarian leadership.' This style of management has its benefits and downsides. Nevertheless, in a chaotic setting like this one, the most effective alternative is to have a consummate leader, the most experienced member of the group who has access to information that other members of the group cannot access, taking control of the entire execution plan.

Constantly wading through the waters and evaluating the destruction and hazards, Amma instructed everyone to cautiously move towards the ferry. Boats belonging to the Center and local villagers were waiting there, to take everyone across to the mainland. Directions were already given to convert the engineering, biotechnology, and the Ayurveda campuses of the Amrita University and the schools run by the MAM into relief camps.

In order to make the evacuation process safer, and as a precautionary step, Amma instructed us to tie strong *coir* (coconut fiber) ropes from the closest sturdy building around the coconut trees to the ferry and asked everyone to tightly hold on to the rope as they walked. She personally checked that everyone in each family was together before sending them across the river in the boats. She wanted to do this because if they didn't cross together, they might not find each other or know whether their loved ones were safe. The villagers, patients from the NGO's charitable hospital, visitors, and all the animals including the elephants were sent first and finally the residents. Amma was the last person to leave, reaching the mainland after midnight. She stayed in the same building with the refugees.

Starting from day one of the disaster, the volunteers who had now been moved to the university campus across the backwaters cooked 10,000 meals, three times a day, for all those who stayed at the relief camps. AIMS, the MAM's hospital, set up an around-the-clock medical service in each relief camp with a team of doctors, nurses, and paramedics who provided the required medicines and equipment including ambulances, etc. Similar arrangements were made in Nagapattinam, Tamil Nadu, one of hardest-hit areas on the eastern coast of India.

The government established twelve relief centers in the surrounding area to provide emergency relief to evacuees. The MAM provided food, clothes, blankets and around-the-clock medical aid to these centers as well.

For the next few days, the entire village was in tears. The wailing of mothers, husbands, wives, and children of the deceased filled the entire village atmosphere. A mass funeral was conducted. When the fire of the blazing funeral pyres subsided, people were seen sitting in the midst of scattered debris. With the future holding nothing for them, there was deep anguish in their eyes. The gigantic waves swept away all their dreams and desires. An entire village stood empty-handed in front of life completely helpless and devastated.

As a leader who understands both the pain and pleasure of people, Amma's primary effort was to console the people, perhaps the most difficult thing to do after a devastating experience of this magnitude. A natural leader knows how powerless and superfluous words will sound in these moments of deep sorrow. So, for the first few days, besides providing the basic necessities, Amma wholeheartedly participated in the villager's pain. She cried with the people, held them close to her, consoled them, and wiped their tears. All day long, every day, Amma individually met the grief-stricken people and during the nights she was constantly on the phone giving instructions to the volunteers and residents serving at designated areas. Her personal counseling and genuine concern greatly helped the villagers feel safe and hopeful about the future.

An amazing inspirer, Amma relentlessly guided her volunteers through word and deed. Assisted by a huge dedicated team of volunteers, our NGO could complete the temporary shelters for the victims within the short span of nine days, whereas it took the government months.

A week after the tsunami, Amma, who had been staying on the other side of the backwaters in one of the rooms at the university, returned to the spiritual Center. Even though there were no fatalities among the residents, the NGO headquarters was badly affected by the tsunami waves. Almost all the computers and several of the printing machines were damaged. The entire stock of groceries, vegetable and rice were either washed away or spoiled. Withered and dried up plants and trees were seen everywhere. However, Amma was more worried about the wellbeing of those who lost everything, their entire savings and their loved ones, in the tsunami. She was completely focused on how to accelerate the relief and rehabilitation process.

One day, past midnight, my intercom rang. It was Amma. I picked up the receiver. For a few moments Amma was silent. Then she spoke, "It torments my heart to see so much suffering. We should offer something more lasting, more concrete, for people to hold on to and help them rebuild their lives."

After a pause, Amma continued, "They need new houses, boats, fishing nets, medical treatment, and so forth. How do we help?"

I didn't know what to suggest and therefore remained silent. Suddenly Amma said, "We will set aside a hundred crores (US$21 million) for relief and rehabilitation."

Her words blew me away. Any response I had was choked in my throat. When I recovered from the initial shock, I asked her, "Amma, where is the money going to come from?"

In a calm voice Amma answered, "That is not so important. Compassion is the most important thing. There are many good-hearted people in the world. Money will come... The first step is compassion. Let's take that step correctly." Impenetrable was her conviction, and therefore instantaneous was the decision. When we say, 'yes' to a noble vision, based on a higher value, there is no ambiguity or doubt. Decisions and implementations are rapid because you become more oriented on action rather than the result. Action is in the present; the result is the future. When all our energies are focused on the present, the future simply springs forth.

Etienne de Grellet, a Quaker missionary, said, "Suppose you are passing through a new place. While passing through that way, remember this, 'I shall pass this way but once; any good, therefore, that I can do or any kindness that I can show to any human being, or other living beings, let me do it now. Let me not defer nor neglect it, for I shall not pass this way again.'"

There is a beautiful incident in the Mahabharata that substantiates this concept of showing kindness immediately when an opportunity presents itself:

One day Karna, who was known for his charity and generosity, was doing his daily prayers and ablutions in a river. Beside him was a jewel studded golden bowl. Sri Krishna happened to visit Karna around the same time. Curious to know about Karna's steadfastness in charity, Krishna asked Karna to give him the golden bowl as an offering.

Karna, without the least hesitation, reached out for the bowl and gave it to Krishna with his left hand, as his right hand was not clean.

Krishna immediately questioned Karna and reminded him that it is not proper to give gifts or offering with the left hand. (In India, giving a gift, or whatever, with one's left hand is considered inauspicious.)

Karna, with a humble smile, said that he knew the custom very well and gave the following explanation to Krishna: "Whenever you think of a good deed, you have to act on it immediately without a second thought as you really don't know what would happen the very next second. Either your life could end, or greed might consume you, or your intentions might change."

The moment we feel an inner urge to help someone, the moment a compassionate thought arises, we should act on it immediately. If we postpone it even for a second, the mind will get in between and begin to rationalize.

The Tsunami Relief and Rehabilitation Package was announced mid-February 2005. Soon after that, Amma visited the major hit areas of Nagapattinam in Tamil Nadu. Having visited people in a number of temporary shelters and personally listening to their stories of woe, Amma travelled all night to reach our NGO headquarters in Kerala the following morning. Less than 24 hours later, invited by the government of Sri Lanka, Amma left for that country and stayed from February 16 to 19, 2005. More than 30,000 Sri Lankans had been killed by the tsunami, and hundreds of thousands were displaced. Amma pledged US$700,000 (69 million Sri Lankan rupees) for tsunami relief efforts in that country.

As Amma travelled through Sri Lanka, she saw the trail of destruction along the coastline. She visited relief camps in the districts of Ampara and Hambantota.

To the amazement of onlookers, both LTTE soldiers (Tamil Tigers) and soldiers from the opposing Singhalese government appeared in the darshan lines at Ampara. A minister's political secretary, the late Maheswari, was overwhelmed at seeing the two opposing groups in the same place. "It was beyond imagination to see these opposing groups together in Amma's presence. Amma is truly a unifying force, a unique catalyst," she said.

The following excerpt is taken from Amma's speech at the UNAOC Conference held in Shanghai, December 2012. The main theme of the conference was, 'How can Asian and South Pacific societies best contribute to the global conversation on coexistence and engagement between cultures and civilizations?'

Amma said, "It is important to understand that strengthening and unifying our society is not the responsibility of the governments alone. It is the duty of every single human being. If NGOs; small and large-scale businesses; media; and social, cultural and world leaders join hands in building a new society based on values, it will definitely create positive change. Most governments are doing their best to help, but sometimes the funds for grants and loans don't end up reaching the lowest strata of society because the government has to spend so much money on employee salaries. Imagine we are pouring one glass of oil into another glass. If we consecutively pour that oil into 100 more glasses, the last glass will have only a few drops of oil remaining. Similarly, sometimes the money that governments keep aside to assist the poor in the form of grants and loans may not reach deserving people. The government has to spend a great deal of money in the form of employee payment and for holding meetings. This naturally causes delay in the implementation of a project. But, when people come together to selflessly volunteer, more can be done with less money in less time."

With Amma's incomparable leadership, our NGO could accomplish all the tsunami rehabilitation projects we had undertaken. This included providing food, clothes, homes, medical treatment, vocational training, and job opportunities for 2500 people from the affected areas, fishing nets and boats for fishermen, awareness and counseling sessions for over 10,000 children in order to help them get over the emotional shock and water phobia, vocational skill training for the women who lost their husbands at sea or whose husbands no longer wanted to be fishermen, etc. The NGO even gifted hundreds of sewing machines to the women and offered sewing classes.

It should be specially mentioned that Amma herself took the children for swimming lessons in the pool at the NGO headquarters to help them overcome their fear of water. In the village near Amritapuri, several children died in the tsunami. Some women who lost their children had undergone tubal ligation surgery and could not have more children. Amma instructed the doctor's at AIMS Hospital to provide recanalization surgery or in-vitro fertilization to these families in a compassionate gesture that resulted in lessening the trauma of the disaster. Thus, most of these women were able to conceive and have children.

In an inaugural address at a function in Amritapuri after the tsunami, Mr. Oommen Chandy, Kerala Chief Minister, offered praise for the work the NGO accomplished, "Amma's hands of goodness inspired tsunami relief and rehabilitation activities throughout the state. Endowed with a big heart, symbolizing the goodness of the society, Amma has completed the construction of tsunami houses at a fast pace. I don't know how to thank Amma for her offer of unconditional aid and the plethora of services she has rendered. The government has not been able to keep its promise of rehabilitating all the victims before the monsoon. The relief work done by Amma is an example for others."

Most of all, what really helped the people was the personal touch, the compassionate listening, and the infusion of courage and hope to venture out into life again that Amma offered them.

Amma says, "In fact, we are happiest when we are helping others, and we are most alone—lonely—when we are fixated on our own personal problems and desires. When our goals become one with the universal goals, when we understand our role in the universe and act accordingly, nothing can stop us."

We enter "The Flow". Then even the things that seem like obstacles are revealed to be merely stepping-stones to success as we climb the ladder of love and compassion. If we believe in God, a supreme power that oversees everything, try to see experiences, situations and sufferings of people from God's point of view. If you are an atheist, believe in virtuous actions. Help people without any expectations. Both lead us to God, even if we have no faith in a supreme power.

Amma says, "'Does God exist or not?' may be a topic of hot debate. But no atheist can deny the presence of suffering people in the world today. Service to such suffering people is true worship of God. However, God doesn't need anything from us, because God is the giver of everything. In our ignorance, if we think that we offer things to God, it is like showing a candle to the sun and saying, 'I'm sure this light will help you see your path!' If God really expects something of us, it is a heart that would understand the suffering of the poor and downtrodden. Uplift, serve, and be compassionate to them."

Chapter Seventeen

Guidance from Within

A mma says, "When we are walking, if our mind suddenly tells our feet to stop, they will do so. When we are clapping, if our mind tells our hands to stop, they will immediately become still. But if we tell our thoughts to stop, will they listen? No. If we can cultivate the same level of control over our mind as we have over our physical body, this is the goal of meditation."

Arriving at a decision involves a complex process of weighing many conflicting considerations: grappling with multiple options; the brief amount of time available to make the decision; frequent changes in market trends and technology that must be considered; managing and convincing team members, associates, and skilled hands in your team; impact on tangential or peripheral partners, etc. In addition, many unprecedented and uncertain hitches can suddenly arise. This decision-making procedure, based on the conventional method known as analytic cognition, is often mentally tiring, physically exhausting, and an energy draining exercise. These days, intuitive and analytical decision-making, also known as Quasi-Rationality, is gaining more momentum.

If you start examining how you view the world, you will probably find that you, too, often make decisions in ways that violate the logic of economic choice. A slow but steady shift in this prevailing "irrational" decision-making protocol is on the rise. The attempt to incorporate insights from psychology into economics is called behavioral economics, and it seems to be a finely harmonized technique between rational thinking and psychological or intuitive factors. Often, it is a contemplative seeking that moves the decision-maker from effort to effortlessness. Doing is an activity, and undoing reverses that. We must step aside from the whole process and forget it. We must take a break and allow the spontaneous part of our mind to take over. Only then will things start happening.

Corporate managers have depended on cognition or logical analysis as the sole problem solving technique for centuries. Intuitive decision-making, or the use of intuition as a significant tool to find answers for complex problems, is not a new concept although it is new to the corporate world. There are many cultures, particularly Asian civilizations, where intuition plays a major role in seeking answers and finding solutions. To put it more accurately, a good number of professionals in the past were more highly intuitive than cognitive.

Suppose we try to recall an old song. The song is very dear to us, but all our efforts fail to remember the song. We may even feel that the song is on the tip of our tongue. However, none of our normal techniques such as scratching our head, closing our eyes, or pacing back and forth in the room work. Eventually, when all our efforts are found to be futile, we give up and forget all about the song. After a short post lunch nap, before getting out of bed, just for a few moments, we lie on our bed gazing at the ceiling. In that relaxed state, suddenly, out of the blue, the song springs forth.

In this particular experience, the initial efforts to remember the song trigger a tug-of-war between the conscious and subconscious minds. The song is thoroughly known to us. It went into hiding, into the sub-conscious. We have to recover it from there. For that, we should allow a connection to take place between the two minds. The problem is, instead of connecting the two realms, the pressure created by all the effort makes the gap wider. Thus, the remembrance of the 'song,' the solution we are looking for, moves farther and farther away from us. Only in the stillness of the mind will revelations happen. This is exactly what happens when we are lying still on our bed. The anxiety and tension settles, and the 'song' spontaneously materializes.

All the effort we made was actually required. It was needed to lift us to the state of effortlessness. In other words, hard work is vital to reach the point of total relaxation. Only a still mind is capable of giving accurate answers. Human beings have a natural inclination to silence. It's a deep longing. Thus, there is a good chance that intuitive decision-making can be effective, provided we direct our energies through the channel of stillness and quiet.

The exclamation 'Eureka!' is attributed to the ancient Greek scholar Archimedes. He reportedly proclaimed, "Eureka!" when he was in a bath and noticed that the water level was higher than before he climbed in. He suddenly realized this fact when he figured out that the volume of water displaced must be equal to the volume of the part of his body he had submerged. Archimedes had been trying to precisely measure the volume of irregular objects, a previously intractable problem. His newly understood information about water being displaced according to the volume of the item submerged solved the problem. He is said to have been so eager to share his discovery that he leapt out of his bathtub and ran through the streets naked, saying, 'Eureka!'

To understand the source of discovery in the story of Archimedes, the mathematician must have been completely relaxed when he was in the bathtub. Feeling relaxed when we soak in a bathtub is an experience that many of us have had. In that state of total tranquility and peace, the answer that the great scientist had been searching for dawned on him.

According to modern management experts and counselors, the sub-conscious is the source of intuitive decision-making. This could be true from a psychological point of view. However, from a spiritual perspective, the truth is that we really don't know the exact source of intuitive solutions. When the sub-conscious mind is filled with thoughts and emotions, it is not a clear source of right answers. We can only say that these answers come from a place somewhere beyond because the sub-conscious is filled with many subtle, powerful thoughts.

Amma puts it this way, "If we ask a violinist, singer, or a flutist where their music comes from, they will probably say, 'From my heart.' But if we surgically open their heart, will we find any music there? If they say that the music comes from their fingertips or their throat, would music be found if we searched those places? Then from where does music arise? It arises from a place beyond the body and mind. This place is the abode of pure consciousness, the infinite potent power within us. Whether one is a householder, a CEO, or even a political leader, the first thing we need to know is our self. This is true strength. We need to know and accept our own faults, shortcomings and limitations, and then try to overcome them. This is when a true leader is born."

Amma converses in the simplest of language, using the simplest of examples. Sometimes, she may even talk about matters that strike us as insignificant. But when we deliberate upon it, the huge world latent in those small words will manifest itself.

Amma frequently confers with PhDs and scientists about research. She doesn't necessarily use scientific and technological terms in her conversations, but she verbalizes even the most obscure scientific issues in succinct language. She even advises the scientists on the topics of research they should consider. It is amazing to listen to Amma talking with Nobel Laureates about their particular research, with doctors about different traditions of medical treatment, with engineers about various aspects of construction, with lawyers about different facets of a lawsuit, or with managers about the latest trends in management.

Not long ago, Amma met with a group of scientists from around the world who were attending *Amrita Bioquest 2013* at Amrita University. The question was posed about using plants for curing diseases. Amma responded, "I don't know anything. I just give ideas to the researchers." The scientists smiled because they knew the Amrita Biotechnology researchers had recently published a significant scientific paper based on an idea Amma had suggested.

Let me tell you the story as narrated to me by Dr. Ashok Banerjee, formerly senior scientist, Bhabha Atomic Research Center, Mumbai and Dr. Bipin Nair, Dean and Professor, Amrita School of Biotechnology.

One day, the Vice-Chancellor of Amrita University, Dr. Venkat Rangan, Dr. Nair, and Dr. Banerjee went to Amma to discuss certain research issues. During the discussion, Amma enquired about the status of research work at the School of Biotechnology. When they explained that the focus of the research was the mechanisms for delayed wound healing in diabetic patients, Amma eloquently described the traditional remedy of treating wounds with cashew nut shell oil obtained by heating the cashew nut shells.

Although a staunch follower of Amma, her sudden emphasis on the medicinal and healing properties of the cashew nut shell, which is normally considered as 'trash or waste,' and the suggestion to make it a research topic, sounded somewhat insubstantial to Dr. Banerjee. Although he did not express his thoughts to Amma, he told me that he mentally questioned the ingenuity of Amma's idea. However, from past experience the research group knew that Amma's words and thoughts always had gems concealed within.

They immediately procured cashew nut shells from the waste of a cashew factory in Kollam, extracted and purified a compound called Anacardic acid, and demonstrated (for the first time) the direct effect of this compound on a protein that is involved in the healing of wounds. Interestingly, the research shows the compound also had a positive effect on many different forms of cancer. This exciting discovery subsequently resulted in high profile collaborations with the University of California, Berkeley and the Scripps Research Institute, San Diego—both premier research institutes in America. Subsequently, the National Innovation Council of India, headed by Mr. Sam Pitroda, reviewed the research data and strongly recommended this project for funding from the Council of Scientific and Industrial Research, Government of India. Amma's profound, yet simple suggestion about an ostensibly immaterial cashew nut shell helped us to achieve a major breakthrough in a very short period of time. Scientists, otherwise, might have spent years of intense research and large amounts of money on such a discovery. Concluding the narration, Dr. Banerjee said, "I had no idea Amma is also a scientist."

Taking similar suggestions from Amma regarding research, many of the departments at Amrita University are successfully working on research projects that include the use of sensors for rainfall-induced landslide detection, haptic technology for skill development, nano-sciences in the fight against cancer, online educational labs that assess learning, hospital information systems and the use of this data to help society, cyber security, virtual labs, interactive e-learning, etc. Under Amma's direction, scientists are also working on a major project of designing and manufacturing an affordable insulin pump.

I am very hesitant to brand Amma's way of thinking, decision-making and implementing as intuitive. I don't want to go deep into that aspect in this book. But I should say that her approach has an entirely different dimension to it.

The mind is a flow or stream of fragmented thoughts. In order to comprehend the truth behind anything, being one-pointed is essential. Division and disintegration is the very nature of the mind. It cannot remain whole. So much so, it blocks the natural flow of thoughts unless we train the mind to be still and silent. From there emerges intuitive and contemplative thinking.

In his treatise, Chanakya says, "Before you start some work, always ask yourself three questions - why am I doing it, what the results might be, and will I be successful? Only when you think deeply and find satisfactory answers to these questions, should you go ahead."

To 'think deeply' means to move into a meditative silence to focus on meaningful questions, because only when questions are asked correctly, will correct answers come. As Solomon Ibn Gabirol, Hebrew poet and Jewish philosopher said, "A wise man's question contains half the answer."

Studies show that there is only a meager fifty percent success rate in managerial decisions. Conversely, there is an increasing cost involved in the decision-making process. Apprehensive of this alarming situation, scholars at the University of Queensland Business School began exploring the various factors and possibilities that influence which decision-making style managers use and how those decisions could be improved.

All disciplines in an organizational structure have complex steps, divisions and sub-divisions to follow when making a decision. The process is complicated. Most business people are very tense. They are brooding, worried about the outcome. Instead, we should follow the rules of the system meticulously, then relax within.

The words of Kiran Majumdar Shaw, chairperson and managing director of Biocon Limited, come to mind: "Amma's personality is an extraordinary synthesis of overwhelming compassion and an intellectual prowess that will astound anyone."

Chapter Eighteen

Love, the Purest Form of Energy

In response to a reporter's question to Amma as to what her favorite color is, she responded, "The color of the rainbow. It represents love and unity. Even though all the seven colors are distinct, in a rainbow we see them standing together in one-ness. Short-lived as it is, a rainbow still makes everyone so happy. Love is the essential principle behind oneness. And it is love that expresses as the beauty, vitality and attraction of life. Hence, love and life are not two. They are one."

Most of the multinational companies, regardless of size, have little or no faith in love and compassion as operational tools to drive their businesses to success. By way of explanation, feminine qualities are considered a negative feature in business. The misconception is that love and compassion would make people vulnerable to their competitors and customers. Hence, compassion and love in business may sound strange to today's professionals. Nevertheless, expressions such as 'commitment' and 'passion,' which are frequently referred to by business experts in their talks, writings, and conversations, are actually based on energy. The power hidden behind those words is love, without which success and accomplishments are impossible.

Some business consultants perceive love as an outdated concept or theory. They coin new words and phrases so as to impress upon the world that they are teaching something different, a stylish new concept. For example, what people call 'New Age

Philosophy,' or the popular, 'be here now' terminology is not at all new. It is the ancient 'old wine in a new bottle.' The seers of the past had declared this in the Upanishads. One of the scriptural dictums say, '*Eha Atra Iva*' which means, 'Be here and now.' God is here, bliss is here, life is here, in this moment. This is the sum and substance of that scriptural saying. So, though not precisely mentioned, using scientific and technical terms, we can actually find the seed form origin of almost all new and innovative ideas in the ancient scriptures.

Carl Sagan, the popular American science writer said, "For small creatures such as we, the vastness [of the universe] is bearable only through love." Success cannot stand separately. It needs the support of love. We may seem to be going up the ladder of success without the support of love, but we will fail to sustain the upward momentum. Of course, it is up to us to decide whether or not to carry the bright light of love in our hearts as we climb the ladder. But, remember, without the unconditional support of love, the higher we climb, the greater will be the impact of our fall.

Amma explains this theme further, "Love can be compared to a ladder. Most people are at the bottommost rung of the ladder of love. Don't remain there. Keep climbing, one step at a time. Gradually ascend from the lowest rung to the highest, from the lowest, unrefined level of emotion to the highest state of being, the purest form of love. Pure love is the purest form of energy. In that state, love is not an emotion. It is a constant flow of pure awareness and unlimited power. Such love can be compared to our breath. You never say, 'I breathe only in front of my family and relatives, never in front of my enemies and people whom I hate.' No. Wherever you are, whatever you are doing, breathing just happens. In a similar manner, give love to everyone without any difference whatsoever and expect nothing in return. Always remain as a giver, never a taker."

The new generation's interpretation of love seems to be more of a disposable or recyclable emotion. 'Use and throw away disposable love' ideas are new attractions and are being received by our youngsters with much enthusiasm. Recently I met a young man, the son of a rich businessman. In the middle of our conversation he said, "My father has all these weird concepts about business. He believes in appreciating employees, honesty in dealings, giving to those less fortunate, and a whole lot of other old, primitive, irrelevant, and impractical ideals."

From my perspective, the interesting part of the son's point of view is that the father built the business from scratch and fostered it for many years. It was his sweat and blood. I was shocked to hear the young man's insensitive and thoughtless remarks about his father's virtues.

For a moment, his comment silenced me. But I couldn't help but tell him, "No wonder you feel this way. You haven't gone through the pain, struggle, suffering, and austerity that your father had to go through. That makes a huge difference in perception. He understands whereas you don't have the experience to have his rich awareness. Hopefully you will learn from experience."

There is a popular advertisement about gold jewelry. The tagline is 'Old is Gold.' The real gold is love. It is old, new, and ever fresh. As the saying goes, "Love is the most ancient traveller on earth." I would say that the pure energy of love is original, priceless and irreplaceable, because love is the only truth.

Although we hear of incidents of sexual harassment in and out of the workplace, which may seem to demean the inherent power of love, pure love is still an eternal truth and will remain so.

It can never be altered. Amma says, "We cannot ask for a new truth. Two plus two has always been four. Can we change it and make it five? This is impossible. Likewise, truth has already been established. It is unadulterated and unchangeable. It is pure love, our real nature, energy in its purest form."

Our power to be expressive, creative, productive and communicative depends on our capacity to identify with the inner feeling of love, which also determines our happiness and level of peace.

In his autobiography, Charles Darwin says, "I have said that in one respect my mind has changed during the last twenty or thirty years. Up to the age of thirty, or beyond it, poetry of many kinds, such as the works of Milton, Gray, Byron, Wordsworth, Coleridge, and Shelley, gave me great pleasure, and even as a schoolboy I took intense delight in Shakespeare, especially in the historical plays. I have also said that formerly pictures and music gave me great delight. But now for many years I cannot endure to read a line of poetry. I have tried lately to read Shakespeare and found it so intolerably dull that it nauseated me. I have also almost lost my taste for pictures or music. My mind seems to have become a kind of machine for grinding general laws out of large collections of facts. Why this should have caused the atrophy of that part of the brain alone on which the higher tastes depend, I cannot conceive. The loss of these tastes is a loss of happiness. If I had my life to live over again, I would have made a rule to read some poetry and listen to some music at least once every week. The loss of these tastes [for poetry and music] is a loss of happiness, and may possibly be injurious to the intellect and more probably to the moral character by enfeebling the emotional part of our nature."

Though there is no mention of love, presumably Darwin would have either become a loveless person or a man with very little love left in his heart. If a person is unable to enjoy music and poetry, most likely love, too, becomes almost inaccessible for him.

In the name of building businesses, earning wealth, creating a name and fame, and generating power, are we forgetting that love is the greatest power and the most beautiful gift from God? It would be disastrous if love becomes a forgotten language in business and politics. The former is humanity's production head (business) and the latter our protection in-charge (politics). What will be our condition if these two heads of humanity forget the most vital ingredient of existence?

When I say loving and compassionate principles should be integrated into the thoughts and actions of business heads and leaders, I don't mean an emotionally centered love. When love is centered around emotions, it can have a destructive nature to it because emotionally centered love results in unintelligent attachment. With a loss in the power of discrimination, such love can cause more harm than good to the individual and society.

Rather, what I am talking about is a loving and compassionate outlook based on genuine spiritual principles. This means a sincere effort to see things from a broader perspective by employing an acceptable level of equality, respect, recognition, and concern for team members, regardless of their designation and status.

Amma repeatedly asks her team members to discuss options and work together on outcomes, to reach agreement on all decisions. She is particularly wanting research to be inter-disciplinary, certainly for the value of what each academic department or discipline offers to a research solution, but also to encourage scientists throughout the University to learn to work together, to respect each other, to learn from each other. Otherwise, researchers could easily become isolated islands, taking decisions based on their own limited resources. But when forced to collaborate with others for a shared purpose, humility, respectful listening, awareness, and engagement all come into play. Even if we think we know the solution, consensus becomes the method of decision-making, and we must stay open to alternatives and others' points of view.

When it comes to taking a major decision such as investing a huge sum of money in a new business venture or branching out to another city or country, companies may take several months of brainstorming, planning, and negotiating with experts as they weigh the pros and cons. Committees might meet endlessly pondering the questions.

Unlike this cumbersome system, Amma's way is to make sudden changes and implement them immediately. Sometimes, she asks a person to step down from a post and hand over the responsibilities to another person. This can happen anywhere, at any time. Amma takes these decisions in the middle of her road journeys, sitting in parks with hundreds of people sitting around her, by the sidewalk of a road, in a remote village, in an airport, inside the aircraft, or while giving individual attention to the thousands of people who came to attend one of her programs.

For example, the decision to make a change in a certain humanitarian project or at one of the institutions may come in the form of an order, a humble request, or a loving and compassionate interaction while being playful with the team member involved. Whatever it may be, the acceptance level is high. There is no fear of punishment. No disappointment at being demoted, defeated, or pitched out of power. The whole process is so beautiful. It unfolds like the opening up of a bud.

Pointing out the carelessness or lack of dedication of the people or person involved, Amma may seem as if she is upset, unhappy, and pained about the individual and the incident. These mood shifts will be blended with heartfelt moments of love, affection, and counseling about the need to remain constantly alert.

In the middle of the conversation, Amma will cut jokes and even encourage the people around her to share a joke or story. This will produce several rounds of laughter and joyous moments. In short, the whole process of 'hiring and firing' becomes an occasion of great celebration. Thus, Amma transforms a seemingly difficult and unpleasant experience into a memorable one for those who are 'out' and others who are 'in.' This process becomes a meditation, an event that enriches their life.

One first has to touch people's hearts and connect with them before expecting them to change, and it helps to move them with emotion in order to move them to action. Amma understands this truth and is a leader who influences peoples' hearts through love and compassion.

A French woman, a follower of Amma, had the habit of purchasing very costly items. She had cravings for things like fur coats, designer perfume, chic sunglasses, expensive watches, etc. If she couldn't purchase them for some reason, she would become very restless and even lose sleep. Once she came to see Amma in India. The lady stayed in the Center for a month and then returned to Paris. A month later, she sent a letter to Amma.

In the letter, the woman explained her habit of always purchasing very expensive items. She said that after returning home, she became obsessed with the thought of owning a particular brand of watch. But because it was very expensive, she needed to work overtime and be very productive at work. When she had earned enough money to buy the watch, she went to the shop where there were a wide variety of watches. As she looked at the huge price tag of the watch she wanted, she suddenly remembered the orphans, the physically challenged, and the homeless people she had seen during her visit to India as well as Amma's compassionate way of reaching out to them.

She thought, "If I buy this watch, maybe it will give me happiness for some time. But with this money, I can help so many needy people who are struggling from lack of food, clothing, medicine, and proper education. I just need to know the time, and even a €7 watch is enough for that purpose. Shouldn't I utilize this money to try to bring some light into the lives of so many suffering people?" She dropped the idea of buying the costly watch and decided to use the money to help the poor and needy instead.

She concluded the letter by saying, "Thank you, Amma for helping me to reconnect with the love in me. I used to be so full of tension, always thinking about the things that I wanted to buy. I feel a deep sense of joy and contentment that I never experienced before."

Whenever asked about the accomplishments of our NGO, Amma says, "My wealth is the virtuous and goodhearted people on my team. They do everything." Although she is sole inspirer and guide, Amma doesn't take any credit. She has no claims, no attachments. This truly helps people to willingly offer their services to the good causes she stands for.

For me, Amma belongs to a rare species of CEOs, Chief Enlightened Overseers, which means she has no attachment—not Chief Executive Officer, which means exercising authority.

Let me give you an example. Amma has been travelling all over the world since 1987. Every year she alternates trips to the U.S., Europe, Australia, South Asian countries, South America and Africa. During one such trip to the U.S., while she was in New York, Amma stayed the first couple of days in a devotee's penthouse in Manhattan. It was a huge, luxurious apartment. During a press conference at the house, one of the reporters asked Amma, "Look at this luxury apartment, whereas there are homeless people outside." Amma said, "For me the entire world is like a rented place. It is like staying in a hotel. You will stay there for some time, a day or two, and then you will move out. I don't hold on to anything." Amma continued, "Today I stay here. Tomorrow, I will be staying in a dark room at the Manhattan Center. In Europe I stay in the program venues. Most of these places are indoor stadiums. During the two or three days of the program, I stay in the changing rooms of the hall, where there is no ventilation, no proper bathrooms or toilet. I enjoy both."

When we are capable of overseeing, we, in fact, stay above everything, witness everything, and get an enhanced view of everything. This is the state where a leader finds fulfillment.

Amma says, "A genuine leader is a true servant of society. However, in today's world everyone wants to be the king. What will be the condition of a village or country where all the villagers fight to become kings? There will only be chaos and confusion in that society. This is the state of our world today. People only want to be leaders. As a result, there is no one to serve the people. Become a true servant of the people, and you will become a real leader."

Once we realize the essence of selflessness, the way we see it in nature, and make it part and parcel of our life, the only experience we will have is a deep feeling of gratitude. Everything else disappears, and we remain as a humble offering, gratefully accepting all that is sent to us by the universe. This is the point where the feminine and masculine energies meet and become one.

Amma's success is the triumph of pure feminine energy, fine-tuned, and perfectly blended with powerful masculine energy. Amma puts it this way, "The deep feeling of motherhood is disappearing fast from the face of the earth. Not only women, but men also, have to work on their feminine qualities."

Feminine energy is particularly talented at multitasking. Observe a mother. She takes care of her baby, prepares breakfast, collects the laundry, answers the phone, searches for the misplaced TV remote, finds it, and turns the TV on for her older child, all at the same time. Sounds simple, right? Try it and see how well you succeed.

It is difficult to sleep with a child because a child is full of energy. You are tired. You fall asleep as soon as you hit the pillow. But that's when the child wants to play, hear a story, or watch a cartoon. If there is nothing else, he or she wants to have a drink of water or go to the bathroom. A mother can put up with all this. She has the patience, whereas for men, this could be an extremely challenging situation.

Feminine energy also has a flexibility and fluidity that masculine energy lacks. I'm not saying that it is absent in men. It is very much there but dormant. We can certainly awaken that energy and apply it in our day-to-day activities. For example, there are single fathers who incorporate feminine energy to do a wonderful job of raising children alone.

I see this power of feminine energy in Amma, magnified but proportionately blended with the masculine. So, whenever I see

Amma in action, I experience extraordinary energy from this ordinary looking form of Amma.

In her own words, "Purification of the mind and purification of love happens simultaneously. It creates an upward flow of energy, which ultimately takes you to the peak of existence."

Jesus said, "You fools! You are cleaning the cup from the outside. You aren't cleaning the inside. Don't you know the inside of the cup is more useful than the outside?" Each human body is a cup or bowl, and we clean the outside every day by taking a shower. But how many of us clean the inside —the mind, the thoughts, and the inner aspect of life? The Bhagavad Gita describes this as *kshetra* (body) and *kshetragña* (the inner soul). The body is the temple and inner self (soul) is the divinity.

Here is an inspiring quote from Albert Einstein, "A human being is a part of the whole called by us [as the] universe, a part limited in time and space. He experiences himself, his thoughts and feeling as something separated from the rest, a kind of optical delusion of his consciousness. This delusion is a kind of prison for us, restricting us to our personal desires and to affection for a few persons nearest to us. Our task must be to free ourselves from this prison by widening our circle of compassion to embrace all living creatures and the whole of nature in its beauty."

On the contrary, people at large are least concerned about others. Money and power mongers are on the rise. Erosion of values makes things worse. Engrossed in greed and haunted by fear of security, people lead an unhappy life with sorrow gnawing from within.

Survival demands change. If we resist this change, nature will force us to change, which will manifest as natural disasters.

Amma explains, "There are two types of growth, growing up and growing old. Growing up is a journey to maturity, whereas growing old leads you to fear and death. The latter happens to everyone, to all creatures. However, the former happens only to those who have the courage to go beneath the surface of life's experiences and accept change with all openness."

As George Bernard Shaw pointed out, "Progress is impossible without change, and those who cannot change their minds, cannot change anything." In short, a truly beneficial change happens only when there is a shift in our inner consciousness that involves discarding old memories, habits, etc. Without doing the inner work and dispelling the darkness of the past, we only create a false impression that we have changed. In reality we are deluded. We wear that mask of the past and become completely identified with it. We believe we are the mask and may even lead others along the same path. As the scriptures say, "It is like the blind leading the blind." To put it bluntly, we are being pushed to even greater darkness.

Our mind might try to convince us that we are out of the dark chambers of the past, that we have made great strides in emerging from our limitations. Some people simply pretend they have emerged from the past. Others are simply unaware they are still in the past. For those who truly are beyond their limitations and weaknesses, their actions will show that. Only when we make the inner journey from the past to the present can we hope to survive and thrive.

Although the dark clouds of negativities are increasing, an unprejudiced appraisal will show vibrant signs of an awakening, a call for a revival. Sincere efforts leading to an inner transformation are underway. We can do it. In truth, we alone are capable of doing it. We are yet to realize the infinite power within.

Adversities are the most fertile soil for inner growth to take place. It is through struggle and facing dangers courageously that a seed emerges out of the soil and grows into a huge shade-giving tree.

I am reminded of Amma's words, "We normally put cow dung and used tea leaves as manure for a rose plant. From the smelly, so-called dirt, blossoms the beautiful and fragrant rosebud. The plant itself has numerous thorns on it, still the rosebud happily stays on the stem, in the midst of all negative circumstances, spreading its exquisiteness to one and all. In a similar manner, even though everything in the world seems to be going astray, we can and we must grow out of this temporary darkness."

Everything is dynamic and continually changing. There is a true yearning for change, which may be less about fixing a broken world than about bringing values to the forefront. Gradually, some Fortune 500 companies are integrating compassion in their business plans. They are taking steps to be more caring and spiritual. Members of Boards of Directors who wish to act in a socially responsible way are seriously questioning habitually selfish motives of corporates and their insensitivity to people and nature.

So may our passions and compassion go hand in hand. May our thinking be transformed through introspection and meditation. May all energy-dissipating emotions be converted into love, the purest form of energy.